simplestyle

creating relaxed interiors in the contemporary home

Julia Bird

text by Bridget Bodoano photography by Hotze Eisma

Publishing Director: Anne Furniss
Art Director: Mary Evans
Project Editors: Nicki Marshall & Lisa Dyer
Designer: Sue Storey
Illustrator: Bridget Bodoano
Production: Sarah Tucker

This edition first published in 2007 by Quadrille Publishing

ISBN 978 184400 524 6

Printed in Singapore

Contents

Part One

Elements of simple

the simple approach

Simplicity is the essence of contemporary interior style. Creating a blank canvas on which to arrange essential possessions and inject personal touches is the first step toward a calmer, more composed ambience in which to enjoy your home. A simple style approach is about looking at new ways to use space and color, choosing materials and furnishings, and addressing the challenges of storage to design a look that is unfussy, comfortable, and easy to live in and reflects your own individuality.

gold and silver simple glass line and figure organic texture brick and metal

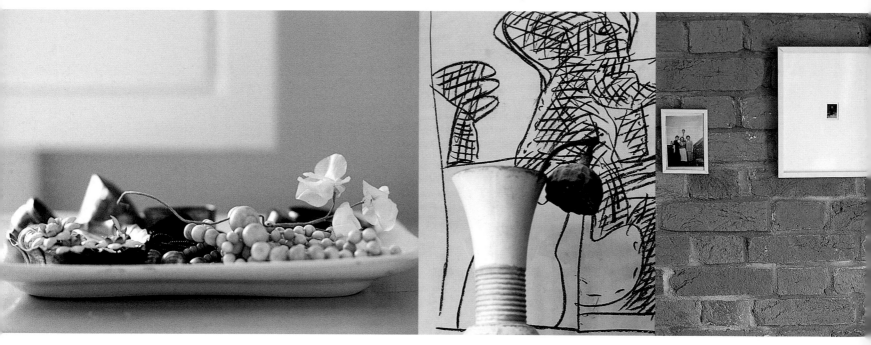

Space is an important element—whether achieved by removing walls for open-plan living or simply by using a pale color to create an illusion of space. Much of the style and feel of an interior relates to the materials and surfaces used throughout. The mellow qualities of existing or reclaimed materials add character. New materials are crisper and smoother, and will sharpen and modernize a setting. Steel and glass add definition, while natural stone and wood bring harmony through color and texture.

crisp linen white and neutral ordered displays blue and white reflective metals

White and neutral colors enhance the feeling of space, bring light and freshness to a room, and provide an unobtrusive backdrop for furnishings. Bolder colors inject life, accent, and contrast. Functional, practical, and hardworking pieces of furniture offer a simple honesty. Colors, surfaces, textiles, and shapes can be chosen to blend into the surroundings or to stand out as features. Combining a mix of styles will help to create an original look. Incorporating extra storage will assist in the

painterly palettes soft and hard-edged fresh florals antique and modern

creation of a clutter-free, streamlined environment and ensure that it remains so. Shelving provides the opportunity to display favorite belongings or collections or to highlight the beauty of a simple arrangement, such as a stack of white china or a row of books. The simple approach is not a fixed style; it encompasses a wide variety of looks, from the strict discipline of white-on-white to the joyous celebration of raw materials. It allows you to put together a style that is both personal and unique.

pattern and plain rough-hewn stone light and space natural wood clean and clear

Right **The open-plan layout of this apartment in a former artist's studio ensures the character of the building is retained and allows an abundance of light to penetrate into every area. Structural pillars and beams have been painted white to simplify the space. The second floor houses the living and kitchen areas, while the bedroom and office are on the first floor.**

space

A desire for more space and light has become an important aspect of contemporary interior design, influencing the way we use and allocate space. The appeal of loft living and the allure of minimalism lies in large, calm spaces and pared-down simplicity, which is a perfect antidote to the fast pace of busy lives. A demand for flexible interiors that can be adapted to accommodate changing lifestyles and needs has also led to a less defined use of rooms. More general living areas have been opened up, so that cooking, eating, relaxing, and even working can all take place within a larger and more sociable space.

Not everyone has the luxury of large amounts of space, but creating a spacious feel in even the tiniest apartment is possible by employing imagination and disciplined control. A simple style approach is as much about achieving a feeling or an illusion of space as it is about maximizing space, and this can be achieved by

careful and considered use of color and materials, together with a paring-down of furniture and other possessions.

A collection of rooms, each with a different function and decorating scheme, can be transformed into a single cohesive space by painting the walls and paintwork a similar color and carrying the same floor surface throughout. Glossy surfaces are more reflective and make a room seem bigger, while painting ceilings in a lighter color than the walls makes them appear higher. Bare floors and walls and a restrained use of furnishings enhance a spacious feel.

Central heating and more sociable ways of living reduce the need for doors between rooms. Open doorways allow light, and the eye, to travel unimpeded throughout the space. Simply removing doors will make a difference, but enlarging a doorway, by widening it or making it floor-to-ceiling height, can make a

Above **Open metal-frame kitchen fixtures and the metal stair rail are entirely in keeping with the commercial origins of the building, as is the wall of cabinets that divides the kitchen and living areas. The use of white, pale gray, and reflective metals keeps this relatively small home spacious, and the skylight above allows even more light to enter the space.**

Left **An otherwise dark
narrow staircase has been
transformed into a
sculptural feature with an
open, stepped side. Not only
does the design allow light
to enter; it also highlights
the beauty of the oak stairs,
which link to the oak floors
and baseboards.**

radical change, and this is easier and less drastic than removing a wall. Raising the height of doorways also gives the illusion of higher ceilings. Freeing up the circulation routes encourages better use of the space as a whole, as rooms that may have been underused become much more accessible.

The desire to maintain the full impact of high ceilings and large areas of floor and windows has led to open-plan living. Structural work, including knocking down walls, building extensions, and opening up roof spaces, creates more space. Opening up the whole of one floor can be dramatic and successful. You will almost certainly acquire a better-lit environment—windows will expose the space to more light during the day, illuminating areas that were previously dark or perhaps never received direct sunlight. Glazed glass roofs or skylights can be installed, allowing light into the center of a home or to brighten dark hallways. Opening up narrow, poorly lit areas,

Right **The doorway to this bedroom has been enlarged, adding a sense of space and height, and giving a more contemporary and unexpected feel. When left open, the custom-built paneled door allows light from both sides to flood into the room.**

such as hallways and staircases, has an immediate effect. Open stairs allow light from above to penetrate to lower floors, or vice versa. Remember to provide areas for storage when reconstructing a space. Dark areas can house utility equipment, bathrooms, or shower cabinets, where natural light is not so necessary.

The demand for housing in cities has resulted in the conversion of redundant warehouses, factories, and offices into loft spaces. Usually bought as a shell, they offer a unique opportunity to radically alter the conventional layout of a home. Instead of the old wood and rough stonework seen in some country properties, original materials, such as brick, concrete, raw wood, metal, and cast iron, have been left in place in lofts and are much admired for their industrial references. Mezzanine levels, sleeping platforms, and open walkways are all ways of retaining the character and open aspect of warehouse buildings, and a desire to emulate

Right **Here, a warm
ambience is derived from
the colors of the exposed
brickwork and raw wood of
the staircase and original
floorboards. Smoother,
paler wood, used for the
table and benches, adds a
calmer, more sophisticated
feel. A full-height floating
partition wall, adorned by
a picture, separates a
dining space from the
kitchen area beyond.**

Left **The charm and character of a small stone English barn has been retained by leaving the beams and roof timbers exposed and keeping the built-in wall around the sleeping area as low as possible. Blue paintwork, seen here on the bed surround, has been used throughout all areas of the home to provide continuity. Its cool color enhances the feeling of space.**

Above **To avoid any loss of space, the whole of this industrial interior has been opened up. An old salvaged staircase, with its warm, raw wood, has been placed in the center of the ground floor to act as a room divider between the living and dining areas.**

this urban style has had a significant influence on how space is defined and used in even the most traditional of homes. In converted barns and country properties, traditional steep roofs and old beams and trusses may be left exposed and galleried sleeping areas can take the place of traditional bedrooms to maximize space. Painting low, beamed ceilings white also increases the feeling of space.

Keep in mind that it is not always possible, desirable, or wise to open up large areas of a house or apartment, particularly if the property is rented, the structure unsuitable, changes are too costly, or it simply does not suit a particular lifestyle. Open-plan living may work well for individuals or couples, but family life usually benefits from some closed-off areas.

Arranging furniture and kitchen fixtures or delineating specific areas often requires some form of division. Solutions include installing floating partitions or using a large cabinet or shelf as a dividing unit. Short, central partition

walls define areas without cutting them off and provide a surface for fixtures and cabinets, as necessary in a kitchen, or for a piece of furniture or a picture. A three-quarters-height wall allows light to enter and provides a place to conceal necessities. For example, a range of kitchen fixtures or an office may be sited in a convenient and discreet position behind a wall, rather than placed conventionally along an outside wall where it may interrupt continuity of line. Kitchens and bathrooms, often arranged in the center of a home, can be designed within a sculptural "pod" or island which enhances the space. Another way to ensure the maximum amount of light and keep spaciousness as the focus is to place all furnishings in the center of a space, leaving the outside edges clear.

Sliding walls, screens, and tall doors enable areas to be closed off into smaller spaces for privacy or a change of function. Tall glass doors can be used to block off areas but keep light flowing through and provide sound insulation.

Right **A low, modern daybed on a slender metal frame and a simple suede-covered cube emphasize the high ceilings and generous proportions of this pared-down minimal interior. A loose, pale linen cover, piles of cushions, and a bare brick fireplace add touches of comfort.**

Floor-to-ceiling doors, either pivoting, sliding, or folding, become part of the structure.

Although cooking, eating, entertaining, and relaxing often take place within a single large space, bedrooms are still considered a haven of peace and privacy. Most people opt for smaller sleeping areas in favor of more space for day-time activities. As a result, bedrooms can be kept quite small or tucked into attics. Storing clothes and personal belongings out of sight in a dressing room, bathroom, or walk-in or built-in closet ensures a calm, restful, and spacious atmosphere. A bed may be positioned in the center of the room, against a partition or floating wall, with space all around the edges.

Working from home is becoming increasingly common; allocating space for work depends on how you work, how much space you need, and who else shares your home. A dedicated home office keeps all work-related matters and materials away from other aspects of life, but if space is scarce, integrate a workstation into a storage system (see page 45) or incorporate it into a partition wall. Opening up space may also create an opportunity to place a work space in a previously unused area. Alternatively, a large, uncluttered living space can be conducive to work, in which case it is sensible to use it during the day and convert it back to a living room when work is finished for the day.

Right **A floating partition wall, complete with the same classical detailing as the rest of the room, allows a bed to be placed away from the outside walls, thus dividing the space in an interesting and unexpected way. Both dramatic visual impact and some privacy are provided.**

Sometimes a space is so beautiful in its own right that it seems a pity to put anything in it. Bare walls and floors and uncovered windows look stunning, especially if the architectural detailing is of high quality. Wherever possible, keep an interior bare, and for minimal impact, use simple, straight-edged furnishings in neutral tones or colors to match the walls. Long, low furniture emphasizes the elegant proportions of a large space and makes a smaller room appear bigger. However seductive the idea of empty space may be, don't compromise on comfort and normal life to keep it that way. Space, whether real or illusory, should be stimulating as well as restful, and lived in, not just admired.

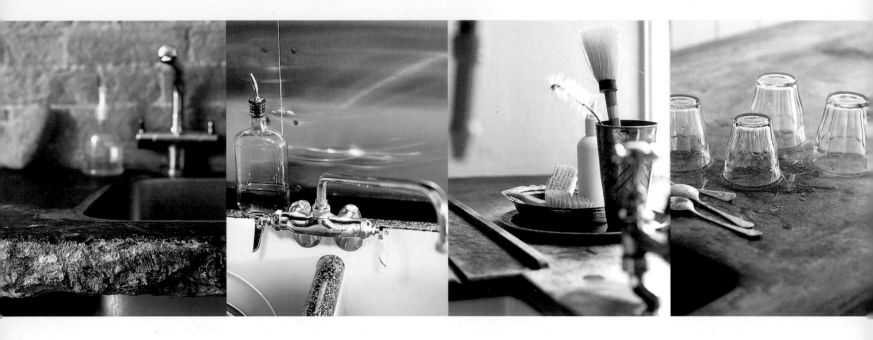

materials

The use and suitability of materials are often linked to the style of a property. Stone flagstones and rough wooden beams in country houses have immense charm and character, while polished wood and paneled walls in period homes contribute to a more sophisticated ambience. Warmer materials benefit from being allowed to stand out against light-colored walls and opened-up spaces.

Industrial buildings and warehouses have a wonderful textural patina of brick, raw solid wood, and dull steel. A palette of exposed brickwork, untreated wood, cast iron, and unpolished metal has lots of character but also a surprising amount of warmth. The terracottas and soft grays of brick harmonize beautifully with the warm tones of thick oak planks and matte surfaces of iron and steel. Adding sharper

and brighter elements, such as stainless steel and glass, gives a space a cleaner, lighter feel. Conversions of newer commercial properties focus on concrete, smooth wood, shiny steel, and galvanized metal, while the new institutional style features rubber and terrazzo flooring, painted metal, and laminates. Architecturally designed homes often contain glass, stainless steel, acrylics, plywood, and veneers. Many traditional materials are now being improved to make them cheaper and easier to use. More precise manufacturing techniques give a sharper look which is well suited to modern living.

If you have an old property with original materials in good condition, and you like them, build a palette of complementary or contrasting materials around them. Remember, there are no rules: it is not imperative to retain original

Left **This kitchen incorporates a varied, yet harmonious collection of materials and styles, including an old-fashioned porcelain sink set in a modern stainless-steel frame and an efficient restaurant-style stove. Practical wall tiles in pale beige complement the terrazzo countertop and work well with the wooden floor and furniture. Mixing light and dark surface tones gives depth and balance to the room.**

Right **A contemporary concrete sink, reminiscent of the old-fashioned stone variety, is integrated here into a countertop with a satin-finish modern faucet. The functional look is completed with plain white backsplash tiles and painted cabinet doors, which allow the concrete surface to stand out.**

materials, nor is it necessary to restrict yourself to traditional or historically accurate ones when considering changes. Existing surfaces can often be stripped out and replaced. In the case of hard-to-remove surfaces, such as flagstones, it may be possible to float a new surface on top. Mixing new and old gives a more modern feel and allows individuality. For example, practical, easy-to-clean surfaces work well in older properties; a salvaged floor may be installed in a modern style of home; introducing materials associated with industrial spaces into a conventional home creates a contemporary look.

The impact of a chosen material depends on how it is used and in what quantity. The floor is likely to be the largest area to be covered, and the choice of flooring has the greatest influence on the look and feel of an interior (see pages 136–41). Blending floors with the walls and structure can create a simple, uniform backdrop. A floor becomes a dramatic and dominant

feature when it is very dark, patterned, or boldly colored. This can work well in an extremely pared-down environment, where a dark floor anchors the space, but can also give coziness in smaller rooms, such as bedrooms.

Polished or painted concrete flooring is new and industrial-looking. When used with modern furniture it looks sophisticated, but it can also seem functional and practical in a family kitchen. Concrete adds an edge to a more contemporary home—even if furniture and fittings are classical, concrete can make the interior feel new.

Stone is now widely used for flooring, as it has the right qualities for a simpler look. It is also suitable for counters and makes unusual—and stunning—sinks and basins. Pale, subtle limestone and soft gray slate are frequently used, with the occasional piece of dark granite or marble for contrast. Composite materials and ceramic and terrazzo tiles combine machine-made precision, clean edges, and more regular

Above **Woods in different finishes work well together, as they have a natural affinity. Here the richness of the old polished chairs and a table with a patinated top contrasts nicely with the duller, paler finish of reclaimed floorboards.**

Right **Wooden planks, used for the kitchen units and a paneled wall, have a natural and characterful finish which is tempered by the streamlined design of the units and the presence of modern stainless-steel appliances and a polished concrete floor. Elsewhere, white walls and paintwork maintain a light feel.**

patterning with the subtle colors of the stone and clay from which most of them derive. Mosaic tiles add texture and a subtle pattern to a simple interior. Handmade and hand-glazed Moroccan versions in variegated colors have individuality and an artistic feel (see page 32). Butting tiles closely together so that only a little grouting is seen gives a more sophisticated look.

Wood is remarkably versatile and available in many guises, from the magnificence of rich, dark, swirly grained varieties to the restrained elegance of pale, subtly marked types. With its natural flexibility, which is kinder to feet, wood makes ideal flooring, and it is quieter underfoot than rigid stone or concrete. Old wooden floors have a highly prized, mellow quality. Wood is excellent for older properties, as it blends in with the surroundings and always looks right, but it can also bring character and warmth to new homes. Parquet is especially elegant, but even simple polished planks add a glow to an interior.

Above **Slate tiles make an ideal flooring material in this converted country barn, as they complement both the style of the building and a lifestyle that involves muddy boots. The addition of a capacious wooden cupboard is a practical and attractive storage solution.**

Right **Enormous original stone flagstones indicate the age and history of a farmhouse. Their worn, irregular surface contains an extraordinary mélange of grays. Combined with white paint, coir-fitted stairs and blue furnishings, they look warm, as well as simple.**

Right Simple wooden stairs and a metal handrail are in tune with the rest of this home, formerly an artist's studio. The mosaic floor, inherited with the space, has been retained. Its texture and sea blue color are enhanced by a geometric pattern picked out in a lighter blue.

Far right **A white-painted floor unites the structural elements of this elegantly proportioned house so that the space and architectural detailing take precedence over the materials. Cornices and moldings provide a subtle hint of decoration when white and maintain a historical reference.**

New wooden floors combine a smooth surface and pristine condition with the natural characteristics of wood and will liven up any space. A traditionally laid floor in solid wood is a worthwhile investment, but inexpensive laminated floors are easier to maintain. Because all wood comes from essentially the same source, even distinctly different varieties harmonize. Mixing them produces a warm medley of tones and textures. Not all wood is attractive enough or of sufficient quality to be left bare, but painting floors, along with walls and any fitted furniture, in a single color or subtle tones of the same shade creates a cohesive background.

Carpeting and flooring materials consisting of natural fibers work well in a neutral environment and will run seamlessly throughout large spaces. Sisal, sea grass, and coir all add warmth and texture. Although of a similar quality to wood, they are a softer-looking alternative, while carpeting is quiet and comfortable underfoot.

Metal plays a more dominant role in interiors than ever before. Stainless steel is particularly popular, especially in kitchens, where it is now seen in worktops, backsplashes, cabinets, and appliances. It is practical and favored for its cool, clean, industrial look. Galvanized metal has a less perfect finish than stainless steel, but weathers beautifully, developing a depth of dull tone, and it withstands a lot of wear and tear. It gives an industrial feel to a home and can be used for staircases and balustrading, shelving, and kitchen units. Zinc has a smooth surface with a depth of greenish gray coloring which develops a subtle, more matte patina with age. It can be wrapped around worktops and tables to provide a functional surface.

Glass is an important component of modern-day architecture, in which large glass panels are used structurally to give a light, elegant feel. Within domestic interiors it has a similar effect. Glass doors and walls divide areas with minimum

Left **Stunningly simple, this washbasin has been fashioned out of a single slender limestone slab. A faucet runs directly out of the wall, allowing the whole unit to meld seamlessly into the surroundings. The look is an intriguing mix of austerity and sophistication.**

impact, and translucent, etched glass filters the light beautifully. It looks fresh and modern and works equally well in all styles of property. Glass can make an older house look startlingly up-to-date and can transform a featureless apartment into a smart, sophisticated environment. Wired safety glass has just the right functional look for contemporary interiors influenced by the loft or industrial style, and it works well with metal, too.

Plastics have the advantage of a consistently even quality, finish, and color and may be molded and formed into curvaceous or sharp-edged shapes. They can be obtained in bright, dense colors or soft, translucent shades. Their use is mainly confined to furniture and accessories, but sheet plastics are also used for backsplashes, screening, and even blinds.

Wallpaper can create a feature in a room. Keeping the style, color, or material similar to the rest of the contents in an interior ensures that the overall effect is simple. The newest ranges combine large-scale patterns with subtle colorings and look effective when they decorate just one wall. Imaginative use can also be made of individual sheets of unusual papers or lengths of fabric. Avoid wallpaper in areas of heavy wear, as it cannot be cleaned easily; place it above a chair rail or in an underused room, such as a guest bedroom, where it will stay clean.

When choosing a surface, pay particular attention to its physical properties. For example, sisal is coarse-textured and will feel rough on bare feet; a gleaming stainless-steel table may look beautiful, but it can be cold and noisy when used. Avoid monotony by combining tones and textures. For example, using only rough and rustic materials can look heavy, so mix in smoother, more refined finishes to lighten and simplify the effect. Similarly, rather than using one color and finish, try to achieve a more subtle and harmonious feel with different textures and lighter and darker tones.

Above **These three examples demonstrate the diversity of natural materials. The rugged characteristics of stone are seen on a zinc-topped shelf, while fibrous Japanese handmade papers, hung on the wall, resemble paneling. Irregular, hand-thrown, glazed ceramic bowls contrast with a dramatically dark and smoothly polished granite surface.**

color

Color plays an important role in creating a look, style, or mood and can be used to unify, highlight, dramatize, and, when necessary, to hide or disguise. Color has the power to change the atmosphere and character of a home. Sometimes a fresh coat of paint is all that is required, but equally the addition of something as simple as a cushion or a throw brings a room to life or makes it more restful. Recognizing that color exists in the most subtle off-white as well as in bold red makes creating a palette for your interior more interesting and satisfying.

With the simple approach, color is most often used to create a composed, discreet background and maintain a feeling of space, but it can also develop and enhance an existing color theme or announce a change of setting. Cool colors, such as blues and greens, give a sense of space and a restful, tranquil feel, which makes them particularly effective choices for bedrooms and bathrooms. The more white a color includes, the more reflective it will be and the greater the feeling of space. Warm colors tend to draw a space inward, making it seem

Above left **A set of modern chairs in bright pink and red brings a splash of color to this country kitchen. Striped red, orange, pink, and beige draperies link to the chairs and floor tones, while a white vinyl tablecloth adds informality and increases the bold effect of the colors.**

Left **Cushions are the only color present in this all-white environment. With covers made from recycled scarves in orange printed silks and backed with a dark brown tweed, they stand out dramatically against minimal surroundings and introduce texture, pattern, and personality.**

Right **In such a pared-down setting, a pair of splendid retro-style chairs with metal frames can be appreciated for their ingenuous, wonderfully curving design, as well as for the clear purity of color and the smooth texture of their fitted upholstered covers.**

Above **The gray of the paint-washed floor is present in both the subdued coloring of the damask upholstered chair and the muted pattern of the woven throw. In a deceptively simple way, the autumnal colors of the throw and the upholstery harmonize well together.**

Left **Old brown leather has a particularly mellow quality, beautifully complemented here by a soft brown velvet seat. These hues, echoed in the bold modern print of a single, large cushion, stand out wonderfully against the white background.**

Above **A restrained palette of neutral colors is derived from the warm pale gray paint of the paneled wall and box seat, combined with the glowing wood of the tabletop and the well-worn paintwork of the wooden chairs.**

more cozy. White is perhaps the ultimate simple color. It looks clean and fresh, reflects maximum light, and provides a perfect antidote to a busy lifestyle. When used for walls and floors, it transforms an interior into a large blank canvas on which a palette of colors, materials, and objects can be arranged.

Many different interpretations of white are available in paint colors, materials, and furnishings (see also pages 142–3 and 191). Brilliant white is tinged with blue and looks wonderfully bright, pristine, and cool, but is also hard and unforgiving and will highlight any imperfections. Brilliant white paint works best in homes with lots of light and good architectural detailing. Glossy white paint, applied to woodwork, is highly reflective and gives an illusion of space in smaller homes.

Some white paints are based on historic colors, which have been produced from natural and often indigenous materials and pigments.

They have a wonderful authenticity, which can evoke an aura of age in even the newest property. Natural or organic paints include beautiful chalky whites that have a "rounded" rather than a stark quality. Hints of the whole spectrum have been added to white to create different shades and moods. Cream, white tinged with yellow, and soft beige, with dashes of brown or green added to white, are useful natural colors. Some are inspired by outdoor elements, such as stone or straw.

A white shell is the easiest starting point for creating a blank canvas, though warmer neutral hues are also good choices. While a room may contain only white-painted surfaces and white objects, the range of colors within those whites can nevertheless form a surprisingly wide palette, ranging from the yellowy whites of old painted wood, through the gray and beige tones typical of many stones, such as marble, to the clean whites of new paint or bleached cotton.

Right **Blue gives a tranquil feel to rooms. Using a strong blue on the walls, paintwork, and bathtub panel makes a white tub, basin, and fixtures appear clean and fresh. The blue woodwork and slate floor run throughout the house, providing continuity. The only other color present is the pale golden brown of wood, which reinforces the use of wood in the room.**

Palettes based on nature and natural materials offer myriad possibilities. The range of colors within natural substances is enormous and the number of colors, shades, and tones present in even one small piece of wood or stone is enough to suggest a whole color scheme. Shades can vary from the richness of dark wood and the speckled gray of granite, to the ecru of natural linen and the pale subtlety of limestone. Pale neutrals, including buffs, beiges, and grays, provide a harmonious ambience when mixed with white, but several different neutrals used together also produce a lively mélange of color that can be further highlighted with the use of textured materials (see pages 134–5).

Most natural materials have an inherent warmth. Raw metal is dark and dull, and only when polished will it attain a cooler look. Similarly linen and cotton in their natural state have a brown or yellow tinge which is cooled and freshened with bleach or sunlight. Worn textiles, wood, and stone have a special color quality that is difficult to reproduce artificially; therefore, old

furniture, linens, and other artifacts are highly prized. Using different tones or shades of the same color throughout the whole of an interior maintain continuity and simplicity, but prevent a space from looking too bland or clinical.

However, it is not essential to keep slavishly to a restrained palette. Natural colors also include a mix of deeper and stronger hues, as well as clear brights. Think of the variety of rich reds, oranges, and greens of vegetables and fruit, or the elusive blues and aquas of sky and sea. These can provide useful accents or saturations of a tone against a white or neutral background. Deeper and stronger colors add life and can change or enhance the character or mood of a room or a whole house, but achieve more impact when used as accents or flashes of color.

The addition of bright colors in the form of cushions, throws, or bed linens will cheer up a neutral environment. Brightly colored chairs or accessories lift a mostly white space, drawing attention to the color but also to the shape or special characteristics of an object. A bold

Above **Here the effect of richly colored Moroccan tiles has deliberately been heightened with a bold use of dense blue and green paint on surrounding items, emphasizing the liveliness and wealth of different tones and shades in the ceramic glazes. The white sink and stainless-steel stove sharpen the look and create a modern feel.**

Left The depth of color and reflective quality in these glazed tiles and traditional ceramics have a painterly feel. Using both blue and green, which share the same intensity of color, is bold and brave. However, the disciplined palette and lack of distractions keep the arrangement simple, as well as dramatic.

Above **Incorporating books into a color scheme is visually effective and disciplined. Books fall easily into color groups, and the whole effect is one of designed organization.**

pattern on a single cushion in a white space can be a focal point, where it will stand out despite its relatively small presence. Build a scheme for the whole interior around a well-loved object, favorite painting, or piece of furniture. While the color of all the objects in a room will have an effect on the surroundings, a white background allows frequent changes of color.

A bold use of color on walls or furnishings can be kept simple by limiting the number of colors used. Using a single color throughout, with variations in shade, tone, intensity, finish, texture, and material, can be dramatic if the color is warm, but also restful and subtle when softer or cooler hues are used. A stronger, more saturated version of the wall or floor color painted on

furniture in the room looks effective. Moroccan tiles, with their myriad variations of intense greenish blues and turquoise, provide a magnificent basis on which to build a color scheme. Isolating them against a light color may make them seem brash and harsh, but applying them within areas of flat color in complementary tones will emphasize them while still keeping them controlled.

A traditionally feminine scheme, with soft chalky colors and a scattering of floral prints, becomes simpler when the prints are monochrome and match the color of the walls, and any other fabrics are in the same solid color. Dark or dense colors will draw a room in—an alternative option is to use these colors to

emphasize the coziness of a small room. Painting a bold color on just one wall of an otherwise monochrome interior provides contrast and drama and may also act as a link to other, smaller amounts of the same color used elsewhere in the space.

Color unifies not only a space but also a disparate group of objects. It can also be used to disguise less-than-perfect features and makes large objects look less obtrusive by blending them into the background. A group of wooden chairs of different styles becomes a uniform set when painted the same color, and a set of matching, but dull, chairs can be enlivened by painting them in varying shades of one color. This treatment works particularly well with fabrics:

several upholstered or slipcovered chairs look more coordinated if the fabrics are similar.

Organizing accessories and necessities by color helps to create a cohesive environment. Magazines often have obligingly consistent white spines and can be placed in orderly piles. Books can be divided into color groups to form a harmonious collection, or glassware or china can be arranged by color for high impact.

Have confidence with colors, and allow them to reflect your personality. Bright, exuberant, extrovert shades can be used in large, well-lit rooms. Painting is the easiest way to experiment with color, as walls, floors, and furniture can easily be painted over again if a color palette or scheme doesn't work out as planned.

furnishings

Simple style is not about perfection or minimalism, but about creating an effortless, uncomplicated, and easy, lived-in look. Homes that reflect the personality and occasional quirkiness of their owners are preferable to an over-considered or self-conscious style, or one that conforms rigidly to furnishings from the same era. Pieces should be simple and functional. Furnishings are not only practical and functional, but also an important component of the overall interior, where they can add character and focus or blend into the background. While clean lines and simplicity contribute to an uncluttered look, a pared-down environment also provides the ideal backdrop for a piece that is a little more decorative, unusual, large, or flamboyant.

Changes in living and working patterns have led to a different approach in how we choose and arrange our furnishings. In order to create a calmer, less cluttered environment, furnishings should work as an edited collection rather than a random selection. Leaving space around a piece

gives it more visual impact. Beautiful, well-designed, good-quality or characterful pieces will be shown to best advantage, and less distinctive items can still work well by virtue of their obvious usefulness or anonymity.

More space and less furniture changes the perception of scale and proportion of an interior; items previously thought too large may look and fit perfectly into a more spacious setting. Clearing away superfluous items, such as fussy upholstered chairs or side tables, will make room for a large piece, such as a sofa, which can then become the central feature of a room. When choosing furniture, eschew the overstuffed and overblown in favor of smarter shapes and tactile fabrics. Consider whether a piece is good enough to create a focus or whether it should be treated or covered in some way to blend more unobtrusively (see page 163). Introduce your best-loved piece into an interior first, and then add other furnishings, examining how they relate and work with each other. This method also

Above left **In a wonderful mix of styles, a colorful piece of ethnic fabric is placed casually over the back of a modern sofa, which is covered in an antique monogrammed linen sheet.**

Above right **The elegant long curves and richly worn leather of an old armchair make it a focal point in a serene interior.**

Above **Both of these chairs are cleaned and restored junk-shop finds. Rather than being treated in the same way, each has been given a separate identity through different fabric choices and methods of covering.**

Left **Undeniably luxurious, this generously sized chaise longue is perfectly complemented and enhanced by a sheepskin cushion. The soft taupe of the cushion blends beautifully with the linen sofa cover and pale gray background wall.**

Right **The exuberant style
of the custom-designed
ironwork chairs and
matching table base adds
curves to the rather austere
surroundings. Moroccan
tiles, embedded into the
tabletop, are also used
elsewhere in the interior
(see page 32). Here the
tiles are set within a wide
greenish gray border to
form a heat-resistant
surface for hot drinks.**

Left **The geometric simplicity of the chairs, table, and lamp is emphasized by their whiteness. Together with the cool blue of the mosaic floor, they allow the tall glass-fronted bookcase to dominate. Control of this eclectic mix of furniture is achieved by keeping functional pieces white and streamlined, which creates a strong working environment in contrast to the warm, lived-in feel of the large cabinet.**

Above **Built-in, high-back seating in a dining area gives a clean, functional look while also dividing and delineating the space. Painted in a color similar to that on the walls, the units become part of the structure. The freestanding oak table has been custom-made to fit into the unit and links with the oak cabinets in the kitchen (not shown).**

gives you an idea of how to use the space and what the circulation routes will be.

With their easy comfort and open look, daybeds are an alternative to sofas. They look inviting and accessible when positioned in the center of the room and can vary from the sleek and low to the generously upholstered. Large sectional sofas, which can be arranged to suit the space, are versatile, make good use of corners, and are useful in small rooms.

Old upholstered chairs are comforting and comfortable. Traditional versions look fresher in a modern environment, but they can be easily updated with loosely fitting slipcovers to work anywhere (see page 165). Covers enable a sofa or chair to be incorporated into a color scheme, either as a contrast or to blend in, and they can be used to disguise a less-than-perfect shape or condition. Casual-fit slipcovers and tie-on

slipcovers are easy to remove for laundering and look suitably simple. A throw or length of patterned fabric will disguise an unattractive piece. Tailored or fitted covers suit either modern furniture or period styles and can emphasize the shape of a handsome piece. Grays and dark browns are practical choices, since they won't show the dirt, which is particularly useful for upholstery that cannot be removed.

Various upholstery fabrics, from the smooth matte finish of felted wool to the crisp textures of natural linen, create different looks. Felted wools look beautiful and tactile, but require special cleaning. Utilitarian cottons, linens, denim, ticking, tough woven cotton, and tight weaves are the most practical and useful solutions. Solid colors are the obvious choice; to introduce a subtle patterning, you could choose a damask, or for a lively effect, a dramatic animal print. The

Above **Natural colors and fibers have an honesty that suits a simple interior. Here, a cushion is fastened with wooden buttons. A stack of fabrics include burlap, mohair, and wool, with bleached cottons and unbleached linens; using off-whites, creams, and beiges allows a layering of textures and tones. Forest green felted wool cleverly disguises a chair.**

natural, neutral colors of linen and cottons add softness and texture without detracting from the space and are ideal for plain curtain panels and shades. Cushions add a finishing touch to living areas and bedrooms and provide an opportunity to use pattern. One large or extravagant cushion in suede, faux fur, or cashmere retains a simple look without compromising on comfort.

Try to eliminate smaller items, such as occasional tables, that constitute "clutter." Wooden chests and carved boxes are popular substitutes and can double up as storage, although a place can always be found for a well-designed, generously sized coffee table.

Large tables not only are a place for dining, entertaining, and conversation but also provide a surface on which to work or where children can play and draw. Tables with a relaxed, rather than a formal look offer more possibilities. A contrast of styles achieves a pleasing balance of modern and old—for example, Arne Jacobsen chairs can be combined with an old country table (see page 88). New designs are straight-edged with a smooth finish, in a range of materials, from dark or very pale wood to metal or glass. Traditional wooden chairs with decorative detailing look casual and characterful, and simple modern designs add a little sophistication.

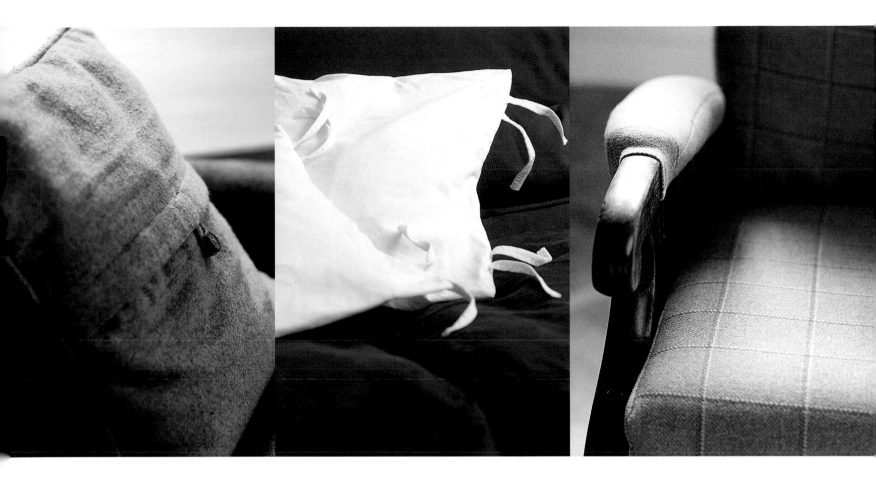

Cabinets with large storage capacities are multifunctional assets, whether they are freestanding or built-in. They can conceal utility equipment, linens, or even an office space. Glass-fronted versions can display objects such as china or glass on the shelves above, while hiding work, toys, or less attractive items in the cupboards below. Their presence can be discreet and subtle or imposing and decorative. Despite its size, a huge armoire in polished wood can look simple when placed in a large, airy space with few other distractions.

Innovative solutions to combine sleeping and storage areas include bed recesses built into a wall of units and cabinets built into headboards or bases. Custom-made headboards can incorporate wiring for lights and recesses to hold books or personal items. Low-level beds on simple wooden bases work well in areas with low ceilings. Iron beds add a decorative, feminine feel to a room; when stripped back to the bare metal, they have a contemporary look. Placing a bed in the center of the room, with storage either incorporated into the unit or provided elsewhere, eliminates the need for such traditional bedroom furniture as chests of drawers. However, an imposing armoire, useful for additional clothes storage, can look right in a simple setting.

Above **Fabrics add tactile texture to an interior. Piped edges and a single button give interest to a neat cushion. White cotton contrasts with a dark sofa, and the cushion cover can be easily removed and laundered to keep it looking fresh. Warm yellow colors of tweed on tailored upholstery blend beautifully with the mellow wood of the chair frame.**

Left **The elegant curves of these 1950s Scandinavian chairs are echoed in a set of hand-carved ethnic stools and a rough-hewn wooden bowl. Warm golden wood tones stand out splendidly and, along with the wood paneling background, help to temper the rigid lines of the stainless-steel table, with its white lacquered top.**

Right **On closer inspection, the center of this whimsical chandelier is a perfectly plain, ordinary spotlight. The unexpected addition of extravagant chandeliers to simple interiors proves that disciplined austerity and pared-down modernism need not be sterile, but benefits from a little romanticism or humor.**

Worn furniture combines an appreciation of the past with a liking for well-used and much-loved items. In addition, the materials and colorings of older or antique pieces have a mellowness and subtlety. Characterful pieces have a strong presence and add substance and personality to an otherwise featureless space.

Contemporary 20th-century design classics have once again found favor. Many mid-century pieces were created at a time when interior design and architecture were very pared down, in contrast to the more decorative styles of the previous era. More prosaic products of this era, including sideboards and storage units, have simple shapes and good-quality materials and workmanship. Newly designed modern furniture looks crisp and fresh. The clean edges and smooth surfaces of shiny metal, glass, wood, plastic, and lacquer contributes an aura of plain simplicity or sophisticated luxury.

Rich colors, rough textures, and organic or irregular shapes of furniture and furnishings add contrast and exuberance, which can lift an otherwise disciplined interior. A single piece of colorful, coarsely woven fabric smooths the sharp edges of a modern sofa, and sensuous curves of a hand-carved chair stand out beautifully against a stark background. The pleasure of favorite and beautiful objects is enhanced in simpler surroundings. Unexpected couplings—of antique and new, romantic and hard-edged, pristine and well worn—work well together and create a unique look and style.

A more relaxed approach to interiors allows for a diverse collection of elements. However, this does not mean that the look is unconsidered. Select pieces for their individual aesthetic qualities and not the fact that they conform to a certain style or scheme. Some furnishings may complement the architectural style of a home, but being historically correct is not essential. Elegant modern furnishings can fit in well with old properties—a contemporary sofa would not look out of place in a barn and, in fact, emphasizes the structure and character of rough walls and wooden beams. Equally, a romantic-style sofa looks stunning set against an exposed brick wall in a converted warehouse.

Above **Beige gray linen draperies with grommets slide onto a length of galvanized piping, demonstrating a streamlined window treatment. Plain fabrics and hardware ensure that the need for comfort and privacy does not detract from a harmonious setting.**

storage

elements of simple

Above **The use of tall doors and paneled wood neatly conceals the function of this wall of closets. In fact, it conceals essential but less aesthetically pleasing items —a washing machine, refrigerator, cleaning equipment, and household files and documents.**

Good storage is as much about organization as about having space. Keeping all evidence of everyday life behind closed doors or cleverly concealed panels is not always necessary and often impossible. Just as some items are best kept hidden, others need to be left on view, either because they are used frequently and need to be accessible or because they are beautiful or well loved and deserve to be on show. Impressive rows of kitchen equipment, shelves of books, and treasured objects provide clues to the owner's interests and personality and can be displayed in a variety of ways. Meanwhile, the more mundane and less visually pleasing necessities of life can remain out of sight.

A varied and imaginative approach helps to maximize the area available for storage. When planning a space, consider the options for built-in storage. Allocating one large well-planned and efficient space to storage is generally more preferable to a random collection of smaller cabinets, shelves, and containers. A whole wall devoted to cabinets may make a room smaller, but the absence of clutter will make it look and feel bigger. In a kitchen, a wall of cabinets can house everything from the washing machine and dishwasher to utensils and food. Space inside a commodious bedroom closet can be maximized with the addition of shelves for storing linens, keepsakes, or even paperwork.

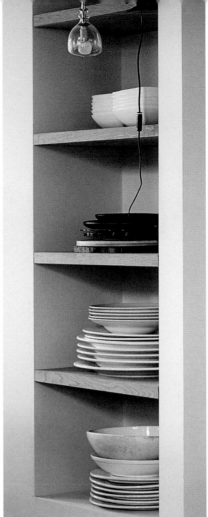

Far left **Here, bright, white space may look serene and disciplined, but full-height doors to the right of the landing, off the stairs, conceal a capacious built-in storage area with spring-loaded closet doors.**

Left **Thick slabs of oak fixed into an alcove with concealed hardware make good use of space. A low-key display of everyday china is conveniently placed to serve the adjacent dining area.**

Efficient home offices, work areas, and entertainment centers may be successfully incorporated into a wall of storage so that they are completely shut away when not in use. A separate floating partition—either floor-to-ceiling height or lower—can contain storage recesses as well as divide and define different areas of a large open-plan scheme. Doors in the same color as the wall will meld into the background, becoming virtually invisible. Alternatively, a wall can become a feature if a contrasting color or finish, such as a dark wood or veneer, is used. Spring-loaded or magnetic door mechanisms allow storage to be concealed behind a discreetly paneled wall.

Storage can be custom-built in alcoves or recesses. Utilizing unused or awkward spaces for storage, such as hallways and under-stair areas, has the added advantage of smoothing out an otherwise uneven or unbalanced space.

Large free-standing cabinets can take the form of magnificent old armoires or plain painted units. Paring down the contents of a room often frees space for a large piece of storage. This can be fitted with extra shelves, rails, or cubbyholes to maximize its usefulness; while keeping belongings safely out of sight, the piece also serves as a featured item in the room's design. Equally effective in living and working areas, kitchens, bedrooms, bathrooms, and hallways,

Left Metal lockers look perfectly at home in this converted artist's studio and provide an unusual alternative to traditional kitchen cupboards. Their gray blue metal finish is echoed in the dining chairs. An open stainless-steel unit provides a work surface as well as useful storage for kitchen equipment.

Right Two cozy-looking bunk beds built into a wall of storage make efficient use of space in this tiny bedroom. The structure creates a charming feature, which evokes the character of the property—a converted barn.

freestanding units can also be used as space dividers and even headboards.

Glass-fronted cabinets combine the functions of storage and display, and so can be used for collections of china, glass, and *objets d'art*. A disparate group of objects placed behind glass doors is more organized than if the pieces were scattered around a room.

Salvaged medical cabinets and gym lockers, usually made of metal, have a sturdy, functional appearance that makes them a novel but useful form of storage. The tall, slim proportions of lockers are suited to small spaces. Ex-library shelving on wheels can be used as room dividers or storage for magazines, books, or

cooking equipment. Catering-style shelf units or metal office systems create a businesslike atmosphere, which is thoroughly in tune with loft living. If space is limited, look for units that have sliding doors, rather than conventional doors, which need extra space to swing open.

Combining storage with seating or bedding maximizes space. Low shelves can be built as seating along a wall, with cabinets underneath. Old settles have generous amounts of stowage beneath their hinged seats, and ship's-style, built-in seating can be custom made with locker space below. Valuable space under a bed can be utilized for storage, either with built-in drawers or with large boxes and baskets on casters.

Above **A discreet collection of gray laminate cupboards, which keep all the necessary kitchen clutter out of sight behind doors, is built into the wall to the left of the sink. On the open stainless-steel shelves with a slate worktop, right, a collection of metal items form a coordinated display. A basic porcelain sink sits on a shelf, with a convenient space below for a galvanized bin on casters.**

Right Old wicker hampers
with leather straps provide
ample, well-aired storage
for linens and off-season
clothes and are ideal for
stowing an ever-growing
accumulation of children's
belongings. They also add
an extra surface on which
to stack woven plastic
hampers filled with items
for daily use.

Beds can be built into a wall or recess, with integrated drawers, cabinets and shelves, and will fit seamlessly into the surroundings.

Floating shelves, which show no visible signs of support (see pages 58 and 209), are eminently suitable for a simple style. They are deep, thick, and surprisingly strong and look modern and pared down. A wall of floating shelves offers a more streamlined way of creating storage and is a feature in itself. Shelves can be dedicated to frequently used necessities, which all members of the household can access. A uniformed collection of buff or white boxes or filing folders helps to organize the contents on the shelves; limiting the choice of storage to only one type will retain a cohesive appearance.

Baskets are characterful, and a large capacious hamper, with or without a lid, can be used to store almost anything. Old, weathered baskets have particularly warm and mellow colors, which vary with age, the material, and the type of weave. A collection, stacked one on top

of the other, enhances the different textures and tones. Fitted with casters, baskets can easily be transported from one area of the home to another, which makes them particularly useful for storing laundry, office files, or children's toys. Traditional shopping baskets with handles make versatile containers, and these too can be easily moved from one location to another. Old leather suitcases, trunks, and hatboxes have a similar appeal and usefulness, and the natural quality of their materials mixes beautifully with wicker hampers. Large wooden chests and boxes, especially ethnic or antique versions, are often valued possessions in their own right—their storage capacity is an added bonus, and they can double up as seating or coffee tables.

Inexpensive plastic containers and crates are available in a huge variety of colors and can be used in an equally great number of ways. Fine-mesh baskets and plastic crates offer storage for pots and pans in a kitchen, household linens in a utility room, or files and equipment in an office.

Above Windowsills can be
utilized in spaces with little
built-in storage. These
white opaque plastic bags
hold bathroom necessities.
They look neat and
organized and ensure that
frequently used items are
easily accessible.

Left **Large shopping baskets, used for storing fabrics and sewing projects, are a casual form of storage under a work table in a bedroom. The tailor's mannequin provides an imaginative way to display a favorite necklace and a pretty embroidered throw.**

Part Two

Simple homes

ordered space

The whole of the first floor of this **smart, modern** townhouse is suffused with light, owing to its **open-plan** layout. The space has been divided with carefully placed walls of varying widths and heights and two tall **pivoting glass doors**. Concrete and metal emphasize the architectural qualities of the space and maintain a serene atmosphere in this ordered and well-disciplined interior. The **white walls**, cool gray floor and **modern furniture** are softened and warmed with wood, **natural linens**, woolen textiles, and the comfort of an open fire.

oversize doors

The restrained tonal palette of whites, grays, and browns established throughout the interior is repeated in the stark animal skull hanging above the fireplace in the living area. The reflective quality of the white walls and the pale, polished concrete floor ensures that none of the light that floods in through the huge windows is wasted. At the entrance to the room, a large glass door is fixed so that it either stands at a 90-degree angle, allowing unimpeded access from the kitchen or closes (very slowly and quietly) to create a more intimate sitting area.

The metal-framed sofa, footstool, and lamp may be uncompromisingly modern, but the presence of fleece cushions, woolen throws, a soft rug, and an old distressed box—which serves as an occasional table—are proof that this is a real home and a place to relax. The fireplace is an elegant, yet functional recess in the wall, with space to store a pleasingly decorative pile of logs. Extending beyond the chimney breast is a low, wide shelf used for displaying paintings, which are propped against the wall. A tall, slim cabinet unit in pale wood, perfectly proportioned for the space, glows gently in the light that filters through a panel of white linen on the otherwise unadorned window.

The orderly group of condiments, above, conforms beautifully to the color specifications of this modern kitchen, as do the gray and beige, speckled terrazzo worktop and the soft beige of the eminently practical tiles. Extra work-surface lighting is provided by circular wall-mounted ceramic fixtures with naked bulbs. A single shelf serves as convenient storage for plates and bowls.

A wall of cabinets in a rich, dark wood veneer, seen left, is an unconventional yet sophisticated solution for storage. The units contrast with the hard-edged practicality of the functional kitchen and reinforce the modern aspect of the interior. All the working parts—sink, stove, refrigerator, and so on—are arranged along one side of the room against a tiled dividing wall.

The wall is open at the top to allow light into the space, while keeping kitchen activities out of sight from the living area beyond. A worktop sits on a stainless-steel framework of open units, which house top-quality pots and pans, a dishwasher, and a large porcelain sink with an impressive water-spray attachment. Bridging the gap between the two walls is a simple, sturdy kitchen table. Updated by the use of pale bleached wood, the table blends perfectly with the concrete floor below. Chairs in warm tones and a friendly shape, along with the use of large paper lampshades above the table, bring a relaxed, lived-in feel to this family kitchen. The interior demonstrates that it is the use of space and the way objects and elements are put together that denote a style, not the style of individual items.

simple   shelves

Adjacent to the kitchen, which already includes a table for family meals, is a larger, more social, dining room. Two more sets of table and chairs—one for grown-ups and one for children, who also use the area for play—are contained within the space. All the chairs have been painted white to unify the medley of styles. The generous amount of daylight flooding through the windows is diffused by white linen panels tied onto a metal rod. Natural linen draperies, framing the room to either side, are threaded through the rod by extra-large grommets and can be pulled across to provide a more intimate setting. A collection of personal objects and mementos is displayed in an unusual manner on a plank of driftwood hung between the deep windows. Thick white shelves along one wall show no visible signs of support; they have been fixed to the wall using concealed battens, which allow them to disappear into the white wall behind. A mixture of books, artifacts, and children's toys shows that this space is used and enjoyed regularly by all the family.

In contrast to the living areas downstairs, the upper floor of the house has a more conventional layout for the bedrooms and bathroom. Space is limited, and although none of the rooms are large, the use of similar elements, including the dark wood veneer, white paintwork, and white, empty walls, ensures a continuity of style and atmosphere. Instead of concrete—which would be cold and unsuitable for upstairs use (see page 140)—a pale oak wooden floor is used throughout to provide a mellow, relaxing atmosphere, well suited to sleeping.

The master bedroom, shown here, is small; but by having the bed placed in the center, the edges of the room are left free and a sense of space is created. Facing the window is the bed, concealed behind a wall into which extra storage has been incorporated (see pages 41, 44-9, 106 and 206). A large wardrobe and drawers for clothes storage are all that is visible on entering the room. The furniture and wall, which also doubles as a headboard, are in the same rich wood veneer as used in the kitchen. Wiring is concealed within the structure, and the top edge is used as a shelf to hold bedside reading matter and an adjustable lamp.

The other walls are left free of decoration, except for a row of Shaker-style pegs hung with a restrained collection of bags and clothes. The impression is of one single structure comprising wall, bed, and storage, which literally forms the centerpiece of the room.

The white-only walls and floors in this turn-of-the-century townhouse form a large blank canvas for a delightfully **artistic composition** of furniture, artifacts, and treasures. The contents are linked by a strict, but wonderfully muted palette of **earth tones** and accented with the bold and unexpected use of **leopard-print fabric**, animal-skin rugs, and large modern paintings. **Organic shapes**, wood in its raw and polished state, stone, and old metal form the elements of an intriguing mix of ethnic, industrial, and Arts and Crafts influences to create an interior that has a touch of **modernity** and a hint of the **bohemian**.

new ethnic

animal prints on white

In a very white interior painting one feature in matte black provides an immediate focus. Here, the stark color of the fireplace also emphasizes the room's elegant proportions and allows for the use of a number of other bold elements. The leather chair echoes the dark color but, along with the tall floor lamp, creates a very modern look, allowing an integration of two distinct styles within the room. An old chest, painted white to fade into the background, sits in the corner and works well beside the chair and lamp, which are linked by their clean lines and uncomplicated functionality.

White draperies give privacy and warmth without detracting from the contents of the room. The skin rug and the animal-print fabric on the daybed are an intriguing mix of ethnic simplicity and contemporary style when seen in juxtaposition with the other distinct features. Their tactile quality introduces softness and comfort to the rather stark interior, and their colors echo the palette for the room, bringing the whole cornucopia of styles together. Even the paintings and objects on the mantelpiece conform to the rigors of the dramatically restrained, monochromatic scheme.

natural ethnic details

Placing a low cabinet in the center of the living room, where its roughly painted back doubles as a backrest for the daybed, frees up more wall space, and maintains the aura of uncluttered calm. The large bookcase could easily have dominated the room, but its white paintwork blends with the walls and turns the books into a decorative display. Similarly, the white frames of a modular collection of small paintings highlight the artworks. An old sack is used as an unusual cushion cover on the leopard-print sofa.

Above, ordinary screws provide support for treasured prints, with their decorative, orientally inspired frames. The old industrial lamps, found at a local antique store, have retained their weathered patina to give a sense of history to the space. Bark paintings, clipped in place vertically along one kitchen wall, also have a wonderful patina, and their patterns pick up the rich colors of the leopard print used on the sofa. The sculptural simplicity of several handmade wooden bowls, in which fossilized corals are displayed, is enhanced by arranging the bowls individually. Against the simplicity of the color palette and the pale walls and floors of the space, the details create an artistic feel that permeates the entire home.

No window treatment detracts from the splendor of these French doors, see far left, which almost fills the entire end wall of the dining room. As in the rest of the house, the amount of furniture is kept to a minimum, and the white simplicity of the walls and floor allows the contents of the room to stand out. The soft, well-worn outlines of the rustic benches and the intricate curves of a carved stool are highlighted in the glow of light. Two old pub tables have been pushed together

to make one large dining table, which blends perfectly happily with the rush-seated chairs and old, dark wood bench. The industrial scale of the hanging lamps complements the proportions of the room, as do the modern paintings, which echo the colors of the wood, stone, and metal.

The design of the fireplace is centered around the graceful curves of stone masonry found in an architectural salvage yard. Pieces have been set into the square chimney breast to form an unusual high-level fireplace. A log store supply is recessed below, at floor level. Two more pieces of salvaged stone have been used as brackets to support a zinc shelf in the kitchen, see above. The organic nature of this feature provides a rustic contrast to the hard-edged efficiency of the rest of the room, notably the stove and the inexpensive kitchen units.

new ethnic 69

Limited space in the powder room on the left required a tiny basin to be positioned in the hallway. Handy for gardeners and playing children, the basin is small enough to be a discreet presence and doesn't look out of place in its bright white surroundings.

Although the downstairs floor is painted concrete, something softer, quieter, and warmer was required for use on the stairs and in the bedrooms. The glowing color and natural texture of herringbone-weave coir—seen here kept in place on the stairs with slender metal rods—is in harmony with the rest of the house.

Light is allowed into an upstairs bathroom, seen right, via glazed skylights and the doors have been fitted with etched glass. The small space has been cleverly divided using a freestanding wall, behind which are the shower and toilet. The wall also provides space for two porcelain sinks fixed onto simple metal brackets. Pipework is contained within the structure, and the tiled surface incorporates recesses for soap and toothbrushes. A quaint galvanized metal lamp and a small wooden stool add a little nonclinical relief.

A 1970s bungalow with a **1950s flavor** invites colorful and comfortable relaxed living. The collection of furniture includes **design classics** in a mix of retro, modern, and industrial styles. Here the atmosphere is **deceptively casual**, with much-loved possessions carefully arranged and displayed, but the emphasis is on use and relaxation rather than stylistic rigor. **Texture and pattern** are introduced through a collection of Japanese papers, inventively used as wallcoverings, and furnishing fabrics. The reds, **oranges, and warm browns** are typical of the 1950s, as are the straight-edged shapes. Orderly comfort is enhanced by **practical furniture** and fixtures for a home that is lived in and loved.

relaxed retro

These curvaceous, molded plywood dining chairs by Charles and Ray Eames, highly popular in the 1950s, appear here in a wide range of colors and finishes. They have been allowed to retain their character and their history, which gives them an easy, relaxed look that softens the hard, shiny metal of the two modern tables. The tables, which can be pushed together for large gatherings, look less dominant than a single long table and suit the scale of this small dining area, which opens directly from the living room.

Although elsewhere there are colorful collections of china, the decision to display only white pieces emphasizes the stark simplicity of the salvaged metal medical cabinet, but without detracting from the warm, glowing colors of the chairs.

rows of long shelves

No single style dominates or dictates the look of the kitchen, although the steel cabinets and the stove possess many of the characteristics associated with functional kitchen design of the 1950s and early 1960s. The stainless steel cabinets are from a medical suppliers dealer and fit in unobtrusively among the assortment of styles in this crowded, but disciplined space. A set of sturdy wooden shelves provides easy access to frequently used china and glassware and includes a display area for favorite items and collectibles. Practical, easy-to-clean ceramic floor tiles, an old, speckled enamel double sink and a country-style wooden table—which doubles up as a work surface—all contribute to the easygoing mood. The simplicity lies in practicality and lack of fussy detail, rather than in pared-down austerity. The catering-sized stove and modern, businesslike range hood reveal a pleasure in cooking that overcomes stylish rigor.

versatile sofas

With its modern shape and construction, the sectional sofa is both practical and versatile. The slipcovers are made from antique linen sheets and soften the impact of this vast structure, which fills up most of the room. Small animal-hide cushions and a rug add a touch of luxury, and lengths of ethnic fabric draped casually over the back of the sofa introduce pattern, texture, and color. Although of different styles and eras, the fabric throws echo the warm tones and patterns of some of the 1950s retro items.

Like much of the furniture in the house, the white-painted bookshelves (with predominantly white contents) were not originally designed for domestic use, but came from a library and can easily be moved around on their large casters. A single pair of candlesticks and a huge mirror stand on a long, low sideboard behind the sofa. With its distressed glass, the mirror adds character, light, and an illusion of space to the simply furnished room. The textiles, animal skins, and small sculptures are in the same warm tones as the floor, cabinet, mirror, and door frames, creating harmony among a mixture of styles.

Sheets of woven fibrous paper pinned to a wall add texture to the bedroom. Less permanent than wallpaper—and much more adventurous—the papers can easily be removed when it is time for a change. Bed linen, in shades of light lavender with a gray bedspread, and pillows in lavender ticking and gray, harmonize with the dry, grassy color of the wall papers and create layers of subtle tonal texturing on the bed. The elegant retro bedside lamp stands on a 1960s table beside an Art Deco-style clock, proving how well simple classic designs can work together in a space. Although the wire-mesh chair, see right, is a classic 1950s design, the light-filtering, woven-fiber blinds and the fiber papers create an overall Japanese effect.

woven fiber blinds

color in geometric designs

The style of furniture in this bedroom, typified by the cabinet and chest of drawers, seen left, was for a time considered old-fashioned and undesirable, but it is now much in demand for its simple, elegant design and the high quality of craftsmanship used in its production. The bedspread has a simple geometric design, and the rug contains all the colors used throughout the interior in a paint-box design. Both pieces of furniture are from the same era and make the room look cozy and lived-in. The lamp could be retro or contemporary, as the drum-shaped lampshade design is going through a fashion resurgence. However, with the two main items of furniture placed closely together and fussy extras avoided, the overall effect is simple and contemporary, rather than faithfully retro. In the bathroom, the combination of the mosaic-tiled bathtub and surround, the tiled floor, matchstick-boarded walls, and a large metal pitcher, and wooden bench creates an ambience that is definitely more bathhouse than boudoir. The neutral colors add a subtle warmth, and with the hard edges of a metal medical cabinet and a metal-framed mirror, there is an impression of disciplined ease.

urban country

White is the common factor that **unites the elements** within this country-feel townhouse. Freestanding cabinets are used as walls to provide both privacy and extra storage, and the furniture and fixtures add **charm and personality**. While an office is situated on the first floor, the second floor has been **opened up**, maximizing the light and emphasizing the **feeling of space**, and the kitchen, bathroom, and bedrooms are housed on the third floor. This area is dedicated to relaxing, entertaining, socializing, and playing. Sociability is the key to the design of the space, with living and dining areas divided by a single tall cabinet. Any austerity implied by the white-painted floorboards and unadorned walls is dispelled by an emphasis on communal activity. This is an **easygoing** approach to **family living**.

The dazzling brightness of the interior is tempered by the presence of an oversized comfortable sofa, two restored and re-covered old chairs, and a contented cat. In the uncluttered seating area at one end of this large, open space, exuberant zebra stripes suggest a style that is more relaxed than it may at first appear. The ordinary wooden floorboards have been painted a glossy white to withstand the wear and tear of family life with young children, but they are still reassuringly worn. A pure white table with slender legs sits underneath a large window and supports an elegant, arching table lamp and a delicate glass vase.

There are no curtains, and the light is diffused through swing-back fabric shutters of fine, white linen threaded onto metal rods. None of the furniture conforms to a single style, and all pieces are covered in various textures of neutral fabrics. However, with the pure white background, the overall impression is undeniably simple. The stairs and banisters, above, leading to the kitchen and bedrooms have also been painted white, leaving only the dark metal of the balusters, which are in a traditional Dutch style.

The whole of the second floor has been opened up to create a spacious living and dining room, well suited to family life. To divide the different functions of the area, a large white cabinet has been used instead of a wall, allowing light to reach into all spaces and creating a more sociable atmosphere. Glassware and white china are stored in the glass-fronted top half of the cabinet, while children's toys are stowed away out of sight in the cabinets underneath.

Rows of chairs—a Danish design classic by Arne Jacobsen—are placed on either side of a simple, country-style wooden table and contrast with the charming selection of small, child-sized chairs. An oversized bulb light hangs over the table, and an old galvanized water butt acts as storage for toys and unwelcome clutter. The old wooden bench serves as the children's table and provides a convenient place for small (and large) people to stand in order to draw on the large chalkboard or pin up a favorite picture. In the absence of a fireplace or other distinguishing feature, the chalkboard acts as a focus and brings personality and a little humor into the space. White fabric shutters are also used here to maintain the strict discipline of the simple white shell, in which a charming collection of furniture is allowed to stand out.

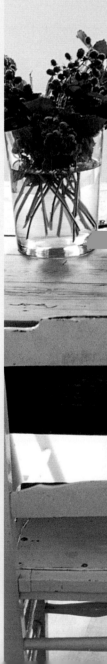

concrete surfaces

A warm wooden table and old painted café chairs evoke a country-kitchen feel in the kitchen/dining room on the third floor of the townhouse. Pale, wooden floor planks warm up the cool practicality of the tiled walls and stainless steel oven. The sink and countertops have been cast in concrete and sit on plain, white-painted cabinets (see page 202–3). Along with the full-height tiled walls and the round metal lights, the concrete creates an efficient atmosphere in which any chef would feel at home.

Domestic appliances, including the washing machine, dishwasher, dryer, and cleaning equipment, along with all the other unsightly kitchen paraphernalia, are stored behind paneled doors in a whole wall of cabinets behind the table (not shown). The adjustable hanging lamp above the table is functional and modern, and sharpens up the rustic edges of the table and chairs. Below each window, and above the radiators, a shelf has been built, which can also be used as seating. Space-saving, double-hinged, wooden shutters have been custom-built to fit the windows and maintain the clean lines of the interior.

The country look extends to the bathroom, where an old, battered marble sink, with its characterful reconditioned antique faucets, is built into rustic, wooden cupboards in a mixture of reclaimed and new wood. A collection of old-fashioned hinges and knobs adorns the cupboards, which, along with the wood, have been painted white to keep a clean, simple look. The exception is the rectangular mirror frame, which has been painted a warm, pale gray to complement the colors of the marble basin.

A freestanding enamel bathtub has been stripped down to bare metal on the outside and stands on matte gray painted tiles against a wall of white glazed tiles. The shower curtain is hung from a ring of bare metal above the bathtub and the European-style faucet and shower attachment provides the water supply. Since the window overlooks the street, it has been fitted with frosted glass for privacy.

marble and wood

white wooden paneling

Wooden paneling adds character to the bedroom, and the walls, floor, and paintwork are all white. A bed base has been covered in a textured woven fabric to create a short bed skirt and conceal the old box spring. The feet of the bed are shiny metal, in contrast to the soft, worn patina of the painted floor. Two small bedside tables have been decorated with silver paint to coordinate with the small metal lamps. The soft mushroom shade of the bed linen, the only color in the room, gives a relaxed and restful air. A glass paneled door leads to a walk-in closet, so there is no need for any extra furniture in this fairly small space. The swing-back fabric shutters (see pages 87-8 and 195) used throughout the house are also evident here; they provide privacy, but can be opened to make the most of the view.

The rich dark tones of polished wood add a touch of luxury and sophistication to the **disciplined elegance** of this classically proportioned interior. Understated and definitely grown-up, the large townhouse has **high ceilings and tall windows**, which give a wonderful sense of **space and light**, and are teamed with flawless, solid parquet on the first floor. The straight lines and bold shapes of modern furniture are tempered with **soft textures** in dark charcoal fabrics, the blue-black sheen of pony hide, and the curves of hand-carved **ethnic furniture**. Cool efficiency is combined with understated elegance for comfort in a minimalist, yet sumptuous setting for **gracious living**.

modern classic

simple comfort

The classical details of the wall moldings and the elegant fireplace lend an air of opulence to the living room that is heightened by the use of lush, tactile fabrics, such as the pony hide on the large footstool, and the introduction of an intriguing, decorative candelabra. Opulence can be simple if, as here, the walls are unobtrusive and the furnishings are grouped together and consist of plain, but elegant shapes, with materials restricted to those of similar color intensity. The large, modern sofas are covered in a charcoal woolen fabric, which is also used for the cushions to maintain an understated look. There are no artworks on the walls, but the discreet gold

frame of the mirror above the fireplace, appropriate to the classical features of the surroundings, adorns the room while maintaining the dramatic simplicity. Objects on the mantelpiece have been carefully chosen to fall within the selected color palette and complement the bold shapes of the furniture. The floor lamp, to one side of the fireplace, is extremely simple and functional, providing necessary light during the evening hours without detracting from the overall look of the room. Rather than making a stylistic statement, the lamp's slender black stand supports a white shade that blends so well with the wall behind that it almost disappears into the background.

modern classic 99

Adjacent to the dining area are two large daybeds with ecru linen slipcovers and cozy fleece cushions. They sit on either side of a wonderfully eccentric carved stool and a simple modern floor lamp. The window with doors opening onto the garden has a set of soft linen Roman shades, which can be adjusted to suit the lighting conditions and will cover the doors when not in use.

To open up the whole space and make the most of the high ceilings, with their classical molded details, the wall beyond the relaxation area has been removed and replaced with a row of slender, square-section pillars. Behind these pillars, to the side of the sitting area, a work space has been sited. Contemporary and efficient, it consists of a single worktop along the wall with discreet white storage beneath.

Above the desk, a narrow aluminum shelf carries a collection of favorite photographs and pictures. The sleek desk lamp and the state-of-the-art office chair, given a little extra comfort with a furry cushion, are modern elements. Pale walls and parquet floor unite these two areas for relaxing and working, allowing soft, faintly romantic shades to work well alongside fitted slipcovers, sheepskin, and restrained aluminum fixtures.

tall columns create work space

Sleek and minimal units, incorporating cooktop, oven, and sink, run along one wall of the kitchen space. No handles spoil the smooth lines of the painted doors and drawers. The surfaces and the sink are constructed of polished concrete. Recessed lighting is concealed behind a slender, high-level panel to give light to the worktop area below. Opposite, the same basic design forms an island unit containing more storage and work space. The floor is also polished concrete and extends to the well-appointed dining area in front of a huge window. Only the single child's bentwood chair disobeys the "right-angles-only" rule of the dark wood dining table and chairs. A subtle, and slightly whimsical, wall-mounted sculpture in twisted wire offers a little lively relief.

Roman shades and wood

The rich dark tones of the house are followed through into the bedroom and bathroom. A traditional cast-iron radiator sits neatly in a recess below the window, with the water pipes fully hidden inside the wall cavities to maintain a clean look. Thick flannel wool roman shades in deep charcoal can effectively black out the room, but with the other walls kept white and unadorned, and with crisp white linen on the bed, the impression is still one of light and space. The dark stain of the waxed floorboards is echoed in the dark wooden unit behind the bed, which, when set against the soft gray wall, creates an atmosphere that is warm and intimate. Simple white-shaded lamps, silhouetted beautifully against the dark wall, stand on a specially made narrow unit which extends along the full length of the wall. A recessed shelf at the back hides unsightly cords and plugs. The bed, which is on a dark wood platform, is pushed flush against the headboard unit. A stainless-steel door handle, on which a shirt is hung, echos the lamp stands behind the bed and is in a modern style that complements the pared-down feel of the room.

An ethnic hand-carved chair in dark wood adds a few elegant curves to the perfect lines of the other furniture within the bathroom. Since all the materials in the space are natural, and therefore compatible, the chair harmonizes well in this setting. It sits in front of another old-fashioned radiator, which is again recessed under a window. A long industrial radiator dries towels hanging from the rail above (see page 97). Mirrors on three sides reflect extra light into the interior, with its dark wooden floor and dramatic marble bathtub surround.

A bench has been built alongside the tub to provide a useful area for drying, dressing, and storing towels and robes at bathtime. The bathroom doubles as a dressing room: wall panels behind the bench and bathtub conceal cabinets that are used for storing clothes. The honey-colored veneer of the wood allows the spring-loaded cabinet doors to blend with the warm-colored marble of the basin and also prevents the space from becoming too dark. A pair of basins has been formed by cutting a wedge from a single, slender slab of marble. Minimalist faucets, fixed above, with the pipework hidden behind the wall, enhance the simplicity of the design. A wooden venetian blind provides essential privacy, while filtering the light into this luxurious room.

invisible bathroom storage

The simplicity of this **rustic retreat** lies in the use of raw materials and textures. Its affinity with the **surrounding landscape** is confirmed by the limitless versions of the subtle hues of nature. The grays, blues, and greens of earth, sky, and foliage are reflected in **hand-dyed textiles** and weathered paint. Bare walls, unfinished wood, natural fabrics, and the **honest simplicity** of plain country furniture form the basis of a highly individual style, centered around nature and imbued with a **touch of nostalgia**. A fascinating harmony of the relaxed and the casual, combined with creativity and a delight in the essence of simple country living, is enhanced by an ever-changing supply of **natural decorative objects**.

raw texture

The simplest of storage solutions, from pigeonholes to wonderfully battered old cupboards, house all the kitchenware in this homely kitchen. Samples of dyed linen fabric, in shades of loam and lichen, hang from metal clips on lengths of wire running along the top of the undecorated plaster walls. More fabric is fixed behind a basic wire dish drainer. Elsewhere the walls are mottled with traces of old paint, in contrast to door frames painted pristine white.

In the dining area, the mellow, well-worn wood of the sturdy tables and chairs stands out against the white walls and the old painted floorboards. A narrow table holds a collection of everyday plates and old-fashioned steel cutlery. Beneath, a stout galvanized box is used to store files and papers. The wooden fire surround, made from salvaged wood, rests against the wall where a fireplace was once housed. A pretty romantic chandelier, with its cascade of glass droplets, disguises a functional bulb. An unadorned similar bulb forms the shape of an elemental table lamp. Two wall-mounted candle sconces complete a trio of contrasting light sources which nevertheless work happily together. A length of white muslin, pinned across the window, filters out harsh sunshine when necessary.

Another salvaged fireplace, seen left, rests against the wall to provide a focal point and give the illusion of a real fireplace in the centrally heated living room. In front of the fireplace, wood kindling is placed in an open-weave metal basket as a purely decorative feature. Walls have been painted an aqua-gray and then splattered with a thicker white gesso to give a textured finish. The paint effect complements the bare wood of the ceiling and the roughness of a low painted table, which has been created from a rustic old door.

Traditional gingham checks of the loosely fitting home-made slipcovers look bold and fresh and link the sofa and chairs, although they are of different styles and scales. The walls are relatively uncluttered, but a display of pressed seaweeds, mounted onto individual sheets of paper, has been pinned onto a framed board and propped on the small table that serves as a desk. A quirky task lamp, with long wires that emerge from a metal bar, accompanies an idiosyncratic mix of personal objects.

Coarse-weave fabrics, such as burlap, homespun checks, and antique linens, have been hand dyed in natural vegetable colors to create a highly textured sampling of cushion covers. A semifitted beige linen slipcover on the sofa covers the seat cushions, too, keeping the comfortable, squashy shape in order. Large, plump cushions on top of the sofa are made from linens and ticking that have been dyed to create a rustic look and are stuffed with wool fleece.

A screen behind the sofa consists of old patinated planks of wood joined and hinged to make an unconventional backing board on which pictures and natural objects have been hung. The boards look wonderfully weathered and worn, with several shades of greenish grays revealed through different layers of paint. A single, modern spotlight is fixed to one of the planks, with its cable and plug hidden out of sight around the back. An ordinary round table has been painted to fit in perfectly with the surroundings.

Many of the pieces have been purchased from flea markets or local stores, and finished with an artistic eye to highlight their inherent qualities. The interior achieves a simple style by celebrating the natural rawness of materials and the signs of use and wear, which reveal myriad tones, shades, and textures in every surface.

The bedrooms are calmer, gentler, and more feminine than the other rooms in the home. Blue is the predominant color in the child's bedroom, left, where the white painted bed stands out beautifully against plain, pale blue walls. The bed linens are a mixture of homespun solids, tickings, and checks in a range of hues, from the softest baby blue of the pillows to the deeper blue of the gingham-checked bedspread. On top of an old painted chest is a charming doll's house, which is also painted a complementary blue. The floor is a more mellow color, with residues of blue paint giving it an antique look. In the master bedroom, above, an old metal bedstead is covered in a citrus-yellow, hand-dyed linen and is piled with silk damask and ticking pillows. The wall is painted in the same soft gray as the damask pillow cover and has been decorated with a pattern of delicate white stenciling. A metal ring attached to the ceiling supports a narrow length of delicately embroidered voile, which drapes over both ends of the bed.

natural white

Restrained femininity and **traditional style** combine to create a serene, grown-up atmosphere. Lavish and uncompromising use of white paint achieves an illusion of **endless space** in this small Long Island cottage and draws attention to the elegantly detailed paneling on walls, doors and fireplaces. The walls are kept bare, and the **beautifully proportioned**, traditional sash windows are left uncovered or have **simple white** shutters. The white-on-white of painted furniture, bone china, and slipcovers is combined with a highly **disciplined palette** of the natural rich browns found in **honey-colored leather**, well-polished wood, and a collection of wicker baskets which have been darkened by age.

The bare beams, stripped wooden floor, and coir rug impart a wonderful warmth to this sunny room. Glossy white shutters on the windows can be adjusted, section by section, to control the light and provide privacy. When closed at night, they meld into the walls and become virtually invisible. Glossy white paint, used on all the woodwork, reflects the light, making this small room feel spacious, clean, and bright. The large, comfortable sofa and armchair are covered in white washable cotton, giving a freshly laundered look. A leather armchair varies the texture and adds warmth.

The paneling of the elegant fireplace extends across the wall, losing none of its distinctiveness by being painted white, and kindling for the open fire is kept in a white pot at the edge of the hearth. Two candle holders, four tiny white bowls, and a white-framed round mirror on the mantelpiece are the only ornamentation in the room, except for a tall white lamp. A simple folding bench is used as a coffee table, but can be folded away to increase space. Next to the sofa, a recess in the wall is fitted with floor-to-ceiling bookshelves.

bone china and painted wood

Apart from the bleached pine floorboards, absolutely everything in the dining area is white, including the china on display, the lighting fixtures, and the table decorations. The inexpensive chairs and the plain table have been gloss painted; a basic enameled metal shade hangs above. Light floods in through the sash window, which has been left bare to add to the purity of the space. The use of brilliant white-on-white creates a pristine, scrubbed look, seen on everything from the walls and windows to the shelves and the candlesticks. Cream-colored Wedgwood bone china, seen above, stands out against the slightly cooler tone of the wall. The sturdy design of the shelf and brackets is in sympathy with the rest of the wood detailing.

The kitchen space is small but, with its unadorned windows, full of light. A dining area is separated from the kitchen by a narrow, slender metal table with a slate top. This forms a visual division between the two areas, as well as a physical barrier, and provides storage for a small selection of baskets, including one for storing bottles. Terracotta herb pots conform to the stringency of the color code, and their scale makes them a feature rather than a decoration. A tall cupboard, painted white, is also in keeping with the style of the house and enables less-disciplined clutter to stay safely out of sight. The bowls on top of the cupboard make the room look less austere and much more lived-in. The white sink, countertop, and storage units are practical, unfussy, and unprecious. No attempt has been made to disguise the dishwasher or the 1950s-style stove; instead, the impression is of efficiency and practicality. Above the work surfaces, a single open shelf on graceful brackets holds clear glass and ivory china. A beautiful collection of variously patterned white plates are displayed in an antique rack, far right.

Windows on two sides of a tiny bedroom allow an abundance of light to enter. Once again, simple white shutters have been used; these become part of the unadorned walls when closed. The four-section design of the shutters—with their subtle panel detailing—offers the opportunity to adjust the light levels and create different moods.

A large section of tree trunk, which takes the use of natural materials in this interior to an extreme, makes an intriguing bedside table. This rough, quirky piece contrasts with, and softens, the immaculate look of the room and adds character. Smooth white pebbles, collected from a nearby beach, emphasize the rough texture and interesting patterns of the sawn wood.

The graceful antique sleigh bed takes up most of the space in the bedroom. The smooth, polished wood of the bed adheres to the strict color discipline of the house. An abundance of pillows and the fine, white, antique bed linens complete the picture of calm comfort. A charming, old-fashioned lamp base adds a feminine touch and connects with the polished wood of the bed. As in the rest of the house, a serene atmosphere is maintained with minimal amounts of furniture and the limited palette of white and natural wood.

walk-in storage

A tall country-style chest of drawers, left, has been painted the palest of grays, which allows it to stand out against the whites of the wall, shutters, and door in the bedroom. On top is an antique plate filled with jewelery and treasures. The room remains completely clutter-free, thanks to a walk-in closet leading off the space, which provides storage for clothing, shoes, and accessories. As expected, the bathroom is white, but here the accent color is a gentle natural linen, which complements the pale wood and basketweave. The glass-fronted cabinet contains a suitably restrained collection of toiletries; less visually pleasing items are stored in baskets. A length of natural linen has been fixed around the basin with Velcro for easy laundering. The linen hides the pipework, which would otherwise spoil the clean lines established by the rest of the contents, and creates a useful hidden storage space. A double row of white pegs offers easy accessibility to towels.

This **traditional home** is brought to life with a bold but composed use of color. Walls and furnishings are painted in **chalky shades** of peppermint, sky blue, blushing pink, bright red, and yellow. Although a wide **range of colors** has been used throughout, each of the rooms is based around one main color, with walls and furnishings in similar or complementary shades. The grandeur of high ceilings and tall windows is further enhanced by **romantic furnishings**, gilded mirrors, and chandeliers, but these are combined with **simple country** furniture, much of it restored and given a new life with color. Bare **wooden floors** and a carefully edited selection of furniture, pictures, and possessions allow the colored walls to create ambience without dominating the space.

composed color

All the radiators, exposed pipework, and even the light switches have been painted the same color as the walls in the house so that they blend into the background. This creates a less cluttered look and allows a focus to be created only when it is required. A small checkerboard painting in sky blue and white coordinates beautifully here. The pale wood of the Swedish bench complements the stripped floor, while the soft pinks of the cushions are echoed in the bold flower painting hanging above. A large dining table (see page 130) is covered with a generous purple gingham-check tablecloth, with the corners tied to the table legs for neatness. The tall windows are uncovered for maximum light and dramatic effect. With its adventurous use of color, the room nevertheless retains a restful ambience, owing to the similar pastel tones in the pinks of the fabrics and the blues of the paintwork—all the colors are echoed in the paintings. The use of pale wood for the floor and furniture creates a simple yet stunning effect.

The glowing pink walls of the living room enhance the grandeur of the black marble fire surround and gilded mirror hanging above. A rather grand, gilded French chair is covered in a delicate cream damask, outlined with bold upholstery tacks. On the mantelpiece, a delightfully eccentric collection of Chinese pots and bouquets of metal foliage add a decorative touch. A black piano harmonizes with the marble of the fireplace and connects with the color of the picture frames, above. The Swedish country chair looks homey and witty with its brilliant floral-covered seat.

In another, smaller, dining room, see right, the window frames and shutters are painted in bright glossy red, and the walls (not shown) are a strong yellow. The chairs are a lighter red, and the table is luminous tangerine. This riot of color is controlled by a strict adherence to the red–yellow zone of the spectrum and the unity of texture provided by using gloss paint. The decorative nature of the table and wrought-iron chandelier are countered by simple café chairs on a bare floor.

bedroom and study

Two decorative sleigh beds have been painted in a pale sky blue that is only a shade darker than the walls, so that they almost become part of the shell of the room. Their pretty, feminine shape stands out as a feature through the use of bright green gingham covers and vivid pink floral pillowcases, which are in character with the rest of the house. Clip-on lamps are modern and practical, and also demonstrate how successfully the romantic can be mixed with the functional to give a contemporary feel. The stripped wooden surface of an old desk echoes the bare, unpolished wood of the floorboards. The desk's shape has the right combination of straight lines and curves to fit in well with the beds, but its unsophisticated, rustic nature is also appropriate to the pared-down simplicity of the room. A child's oil painting, propped casually against the wall, introduces pattern and links with the mix of homespun checks and country floral bedlinens.

On the ground floor of this **former farmhouse**, the walls dividing the kitchen, dining, and living areas stop short of the edges to allow an all-around **light to penetrate** the space and turn cooking, eating, and relaxing into companionable activities. In order to maximize the space in this way, the library adjacent to the kitchen is closed off with imposing **glazed metal** doors. Color is confined to the **natural hues** of oak, concrete, polished wood, sisal matting, marble, and distressed zinc. The kitchen, library, and small powder room all have concrete tiled floors laid in a **checkerboard pattern**, formed by alternate tiles' being turned at right angles. Upstairs, the area is cleverly divided to create the **illusion of space**, despite sloping ceilings and restricted headroom. The open layout, subdued palette, and minimal use of furniture give a sculptural feel.

open house

A shelf has been built around two sides of this kitchen to provide storage, display, and seating. Keeping the outside walls free of fixtures gives the space an airy feel. All the workings of the kitchen are integrated into a large island unit with a dark gray, shiny marble worktop. Wiring and pipework are concealed beneath the concrete floor, and the large ventilator hood above also incorporates an efficient modern lighting system. The walls and paintwork are pure white, and the splendid windows have been left bare, except for rectangles of fine white fabric nailed to the lower half. Incorporated into the dividing wall between the kitchen and dining areas is an open-fire grill, accessible from both sides. On either side of the grill and recessed into the deep wall, solid, oiled oak shelves offer convenient storage.

marble-topped island unit

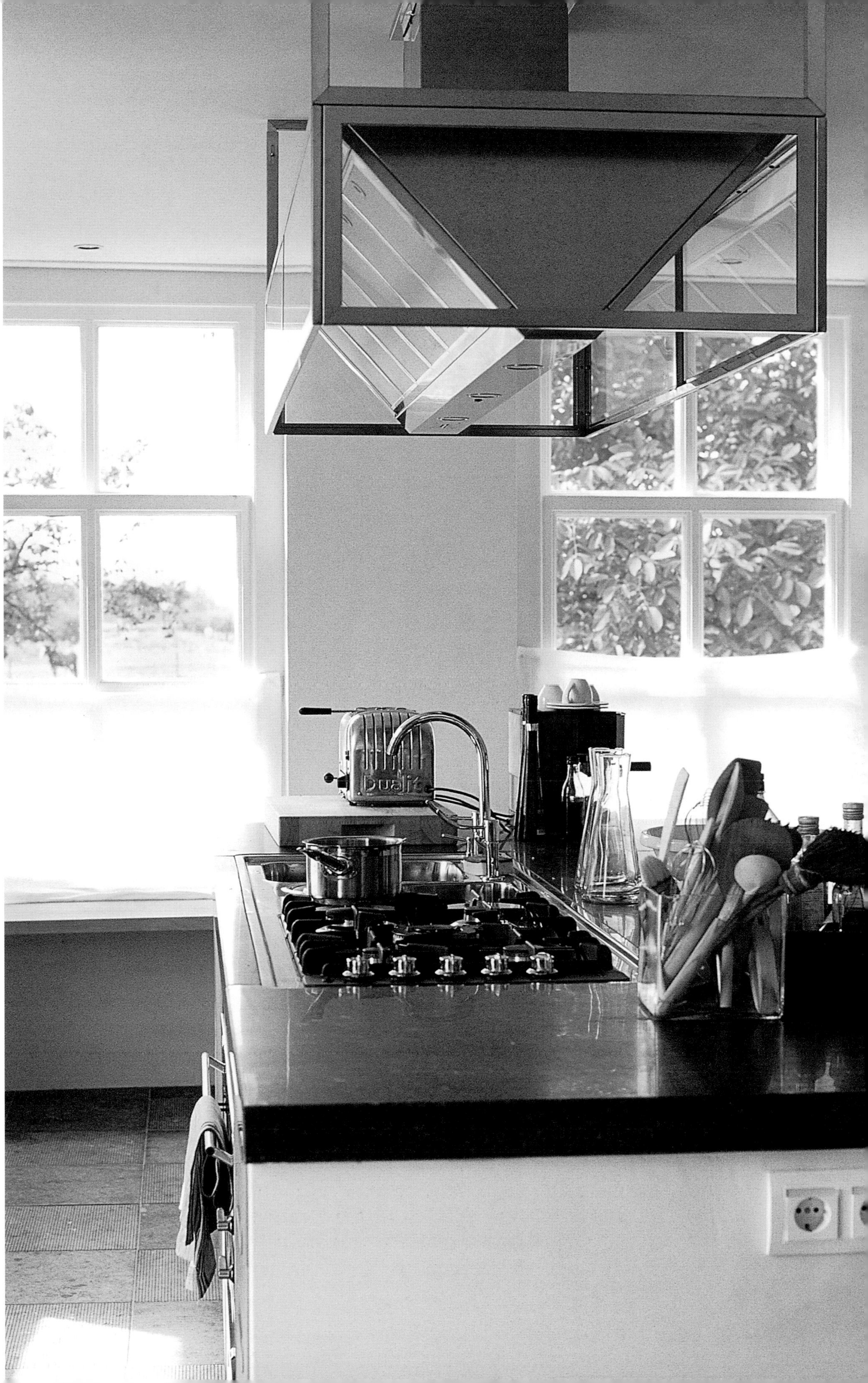

The full effect of the unusual layout, which uses shortened partition walls (see page 181), can be seen here. In more conventional interiors with full-width walls, the light would have been restricted to just one of these two windows. All-day light floods in around the edges of the walls, creating a special atmosphere.

Colors in the room are restricted to natural tones. A large daybed is covered in chocolate-colored brushed cotton. Its clean lines and tailored cover complement the straight, sharp edges of the inexpensive occasional table, which has been paint-washed and then finished with a thick layer of varnish and combed to give a textural, ethnic effect. Both pieces of furniture sit on a large sisal rug, edged in gray cotton, which adds warmth and texture to the surroundings.

The floor lamp is a slim metal rod topped with a tiny shade. Though all the outside walls are white, the wall directly behind the daybed has been painted a subtle beige. Since there are no pictures or artifacts, the addition of a little color breaks up the space and makes it more intimate. Beige also emphasizes the architectural structure of the space. The television is on casters and can be moved easily between the different areas.

Another, more traditional sofa is unashamedly comfortable. Its gray brown upholstery looks wonderful against the creamy beige-washed wall. The sculptural, stepped design on one side of the staircase, see right, allows in more light, preventing the stairs from being boxed in, and provides visual variety. Pale oak stairs link with the oak flooring in other areas of the house. The wrought-iron handrail, supported on small, discreet brackets, is slender and elegant with shepherd's crook finials.

The dining room, see above, has immediate access to the kitchen, so there is no need for any furniture other than the table and chairs. The dark hardwood, country-style dining table comes from India, but the rough-and-ready surface has been polished to make it smooth and bring out the rich tones of the wood. Michael Thonet bentwood chairs have darkened with age and look loved and cared for. The pale oak floor has been sealed with a matte finish and the baseboard adds a modern-looking touch to the edges of the floor.

This tiny room in the eaves makes maximum use of all the space, despite sloping ceilings. Beams have been left exposed for a little extra height as well as visual interest. The bed is on a specially-made low base to allow for headroom. In order to incorporate a good-sized bathroom into the space and allow natural light into both areas, a low plaster partition has been built, which has a console table on the bed side and a bathtub on the other. The tub is built into a distressed zinc "box" built onto the low wall, which also contains the concealed pipework for the minimal faucets. There is a step up to the bath area, which creates additional storage for pipework. Two porcelain sinks stand on a

cantilevered, distressed-zinc plinth, each with its own mirror and light. Faucets emerge directly from the wall, and the mirrors have been set into the plaster for a sleek look. Both are positioned on the only full-height wall, which provides privacy for the shower behind. Pendant lights have clear glass shades to reflect light; they are suitably functional for a bathroom but add a touch of elegance. Throughout the space the floor is luxurious, honey-colored stone. The bathroom area receives natural daylight and ventilation from the windows, but the use of the low partition wall means that the sleeping area, sited toward the back of the space, still benefits from the window light.

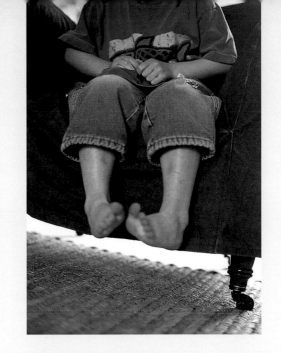

authentic country

The whitewashed walls, exposed beams, and bare floors associated with traditional European **country dwellings** are all present in this farmhouse. A mix of old and new furniture, **workaday fabrics**, natural floors, light walls, and highlights of color enhance the character of this family home. Downstairs, the white walls, oak floors and original **stone flags** form a perfect background for blue denim upholstery, bleached linen curtains, large old cupboards, and brightly colored, modern dining chairs. Upstairs, coir matting and bleached or **painted floorboards** give a warmer feel, with the occasional colored wall and use of boldly striped and checked fabrics. Seasonal variations are subtly provided for, with the addition of double curtains and the comfort of an **open fire** in winter, and a profusion of **sunlight** in summer.

Although all the ingredients of a traditional farmhouse kitchen are present, this room maintains an air of serenity. Warm oak floor is sealed for practicality, and the built-in old-fashioned sink is flanked by wooden draining boards. The country-style cupboards and the freestanding workbench are painted white, with highlights of color provided by small elements within the room. A contemporary feel is achieved through the use of a white (but eminently practical) vinyl table cover and a set of modern chairs. Ivory walls, beams, and door and window frames keep the overall look clean and simple.

Glassware, china, utensils, and food are stored out of sight. Evidence of cooking and preparing food can be seen in the collection of chopping boards behind the sink, a display of kitchen knives on the wall, and stacks of professional-style pots and pans stored on the shelf below the workbench. This is a family kitchen, the hub of the house, and a favorite place for entertaining visitors. The sleek, lacquered plywood chairs in pink and red, based on a classic Scandinavian design, are comfortable for everyday use, yet sophisticated enough for dinner parties. Metal shades hanging above the table are from the local farm supply store. They are inexpensive and can be seen in dairies and outbuildings on farms throughout the English countryside. Instead of paintings or photographs, a large blackboard provides an ever-changing range of impromptu artwork.

With its associations with work- and leisure-wear, denim is the perfect fabric for life in the country. It makes an unusual but practical upholstery material, which is also complemented by the rugged textures of the old flagstones. Casual-fit slipcovers on the chairs and sofa have been washed several times and, like well-loved jeans, look and feel better with age. The infinite variety of shades from the deep indigo of new to the pale whiteness of the well-worn, gives denim its special character, which is here nicely emphasized by the different shapes of the two old chairs. A chesterfield sofa, opposite, looks comfortable and relaxed in its fitted denim cover. The blue cover is easily washable and has developed a charming faded softness over time. A gathered flounce adds a flirtatious look and a

brightens a light space

humorous touch. Squashy cushions with envelope and tied covers continue the blue theme in denim and patterned weaves. As a contrast, another working fabric, blue-and-white striped ticking, has been used for the footstool. The neutral tones of the coir rug blend with the flagstones, and its rough texture is well suited to the character of the home, as is the functional and inexpensive work lamp. Curtains made from linen sheets are sewn to old-fashioned rings and hang from a plain metal rod. In winter, a strip of Velcro stitched to the back of the linen enables a panel of canvas to be attached, providing discreet additional insulation. Keeping the walls, curtains, and table white and using only blue on the upholstery leaves the room light and gives focus to an old dark wooden armoire.

painted wood and nature displays

The surrounding countryside affords a rich supply of found objects. A "nature table" is an old farmhouse table painted in off-white eggshell—a warmer white adds spaciousness without introducing coldness in low-ceilinged farmhouses such as this. Apart from a large white pitcher, the table is kept clear of small clutter in order to maximize the impact of a dramatically large seed head. The dry browns and grays of the plant harmonize with the rich, dark wood of the armoire and the soft gray of the original flagstones.

A large fireplace is set in an inglenook with flagstone-topped benches to each side. The shapely mantel and the bricks forming the sides have been painted white to blend in with the walls; the color also emphasizes the sooty blackness of the fireplace. A monochrome collection of black-and-white photographs stands on the mantelpiece. A side table is painted white, which gives its traditional shape a contemporary feel. Here the table holds piles of books and a single white pitcher of freshly-picked poppy heads.

A traditional metal bed, found in a local antiques shop, has been stripped of its old layers of paint to reveal its surprisingly slender construction. It stands on the bare floor as the centerpiece of the master bedroom. Any austerity suggested by the stark bedstead is softened by the gentle color and warm texture of the bleached floorboards. The red and white of the bold striped ticking curtains is echoed in the stylized floral-print pillowcases and the flower-patterned quilt which acts as a bed skirt. A large, tactile faux fur throw offers extra comfort for chilly nights. An old white linen cloth covers a rather ordinary bedside table. To maintain an uncluttered environment, the pictures and a wooden-framed mirror lean against the walls, rather than being wall-hung, and a convenient walk-in closet keeps clothes and accessories out of sight. Modern bedside lamps on plain metal stems blend comfortably with the surroundings, as does the elegant table lamp on the white worktable which also serves as a diaper-changing area.

gray metal and papered walls

The bathroom makes the most of its country-style atmosphere, small size, and situation away from the rest of the house with a bold use of wallpaper. Its exuberant pattern is a modern design based on seaweed and sea urchin shapes in shades of lilac and gray, enhanced with silver. The rest of the room is, however, strictly limited to shades of white and metal. Tongue-and-groove boarding, painted white, helps to maintain a balance between pattern and plain. An old-fashioned bathtub and basin have reconditioned faucets from the same era, and the basin stands on a newly built, plain paneled cabinet. A glass-fronted cabinet and small washstand were bought locally. Their pretty decorative details are kept in check with the use of white paint and by limiting the material of all accessories to functional metal, which is echoed in the metal lampshade hanging overhead. The washstand is topped with a slab of marble to complement the grays of the wallpaper, the patina of an old galvanized container, and a collection of pebbles and shells.

White floor paint provides a hard-wearing surface for the two young occupants of this bedroom. An old laundry basket, fixed with industrial casters, serves as a large mobile toy box. A red wall and red gingham fabric, in different-sized checks for bedding and curtains, add a cheerful, lively spirit to the room. Red is repeated in the child-sized rush-seated chairs, with the rest of the furniture in the room painted white. The tall wardrobe holds children's clothes, and a wicker hamper keeps other items well out of reach. A small table provides a place for a night light and a propped-up bulletinboard, which is also covered in red gingham.

Curtains hung on metal rings from a plain metal rod are quilted for coziness and generous in length to keep out drafts. The canopy of the four-poster bed is in khaki denim, which is edged and tied to the frame with red string, giving it a tent-like look. Its side panel has two large pockets sewn on the inside to provide a handy storage place for books, teddy bears, and other treasures. A 1950s crib in a traditional style is pleasingly simple with its original paint finish. The children have a separate playroom in the house, where all their essential toys, games, and art materials are stored; in contrast, the bedroom is for sleeping, and its quiet simplicity provides a suitably calm atmosphere.

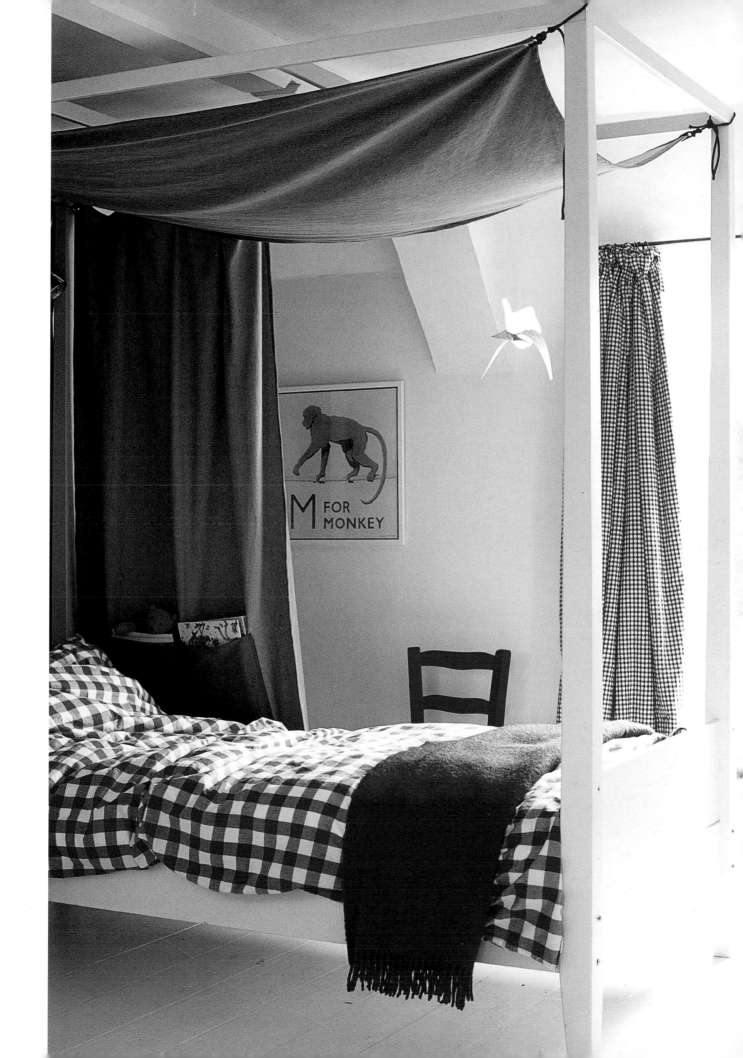

mellowed antique

The warm earth colors and antique furniture create a comfortable, well-established and **timeless ambience** in this elegant country house. Bleached wood and terracotta-tiled floors blend with creamy beige walls and the pinkish tinge of partly stripped doors. The **pared-down furniture** mixes traditional country pieces with soft upholstered fabric in shades of muted raspberry reds and florals. Dusky tones of the **terracotta floor** in the library harmonize with the **faded covers** of old books on the floor-to-ceiling bookshelves. Aged tints and bold geometrics of a display of antique chessboards reflect the **rustic nature** and disciplined qualities of this interior.

The fireplace provides focus in the library. A floral-print chair stands out beautifully against the bare, tiled floor; its bright color adds a contrast to the more muted tones. One wall and the old beamed ceiling (seen reflected in the antique mirror above the mantelpiece) have been painted white to lighten the space and lead on to the living room, shown right. The creamy beige walls of the living room complement the warm red of the sofa and give a restful, luxurious mood. A piece of antique floral fabric draped across the sofa reinforces the color theme and adds femininity. No attempt has been made to repair the damage to the simple fire surround, shown above: function is more important than style in this home. A large, gilded mirror is romantic and reflects more light into the space. No draperies interfere with the elegant proportions of the tall French windows, which open out onto the garden; instead, outdoor shutters are used to provide privacy at night. The 1960s floor lamp is an unexpected addition to this antique-filled interior, but helps to maintain a contemporary feel.

Elegantly proportioned double doors lead from the living room to a small study, seen left. Doors have been partially stripped to leave a wonderful patina of layers of paint and wood, which match the terracotta tiles. The slim framework of the metal trestles corresponds to the slender muntins of the tall window in this light-filled work space. On the desk, piles of magazines have been arranged to exhibit their wittily appropriate checkerboard spines. The kitchen walls, above, are washed with several layers of pinkish terracotta to build up a rich surface in earthy depths of color. This wall color and finish, along with the large kitchen table and stool, would have been a familiar sight in simple rustic dwellings of the past. A stout oak shelf holds a selection of white china, and the inexpensive clip-on lamp illuminates the black terrazzo sink and work surface. The pale, bleached-wood finish of the floor and the plain-fronted cabinets and drawers emphasize the natural grain and character of the material. A large catering-size range looks efficient and practical, and its proportions work perfectly in the space. The ceiling has been painted off-white to reflect light flooding in from a large window.

Space is the main component of this house, which has been formed as a **pale shell** which allows the carefully edited mix of old and modern either to stand out from or to dissolve into the background. **Disciplined and restrained** use of mainly white furnishings has enabled the romanticism of crystal chandeliers and traditional furniture to be successfully combined with the pared-down, stark simplicity of modern style and the **organic shapes** of ethnic and Scandinavian looks. The generous and elegant proportions of the rooms, doors, and windows are enhanced by the **uncluttered environment** and the use of stark white and a pale aqua. Subtle tones and textures are provided by **natural fabrics**, and controlled accents of more saturated hues appear as cushions and floor coverings.

pure and elemental

fireplace and candles

The lower-ground floor, housing the dining, kitchen, and living areas, presents an overall look of white, metal, and wood. A log fire burns on a base of loose bricks laid on top of concrete. Without a grate, and with its old rough bricks, the fireplace is minimal and natural, and offers an area of texture to otherwise plain walls. Together with a decorative display of logs and a wire basket of kindling, the fireplace warms this uncompromisingly minimal space, which serves as the dining room. Concealed lighting, set behind narrow panels at the top of the alcoves on either side of the fire, throws a wash of subtle light down the walls. The sleek, organic curves of the dining chairs—a classic Danish design from 1950—provide a contrast of shape and color and soften the hard edges of the table and bare white walls. A brushed-steel table, with a white-painted wooden top, links with the lampshades hanging above. The large, spun-aluminum lampshades reflect the white and the light, and their scale marks them as a feature rather than an accessory. A collection of votive candles, set into tiny hand-molded porcelain dishes, are arranged on the table. They can be used for candlelight meals in front of the fire, turning this pristine white room into a dramatic space of flickering, warm color.

The furniture in this room is kept long and low to emphasize the high ceilings. Plain linen curtains have been attached to clip-rings and hung from white-painted metal poles, which are discreetly fixed onto the ceiling molding. Two modern daybeds, one with integrated tables that extend on both sides, contrast with the soft, relaxed shape of the sofa. One daybed has a loosely covered feather mattress to pad the shape and add extra comfort when it doubles as a guest bed. Two ottomans, one in thick white linen and the other in creamy beige suede, conform to the low profile of the furniture. The floor and woodwork have been painted white, but the walls are a pale, watery, washed aqua. An open fireplace offers warmth without intruding into the clean lines of the space. Sky blue, silk cushion covers are decorated with a blue print of leaf silhouettes.

The comfort of natural fibers, in the form of textured bedlinen and a warm, pale gray felt rug, contribute to a restful atmosphere in the bedroom. A hint of beige on the walls lessens the starkness of the bare walls and painted floorboards. The shutters are made from Perspex, hinged onto the window frame, which diffuse the light through its milky white translucency. Similarly, the paper bedside lamp gives a soft, intimate light. Two bentwood stools—another classic Scandinavian design—act as

bedside tables. Opposite the end of the bed is another open fireplace (not shown). The bedroom opens into an adjacent walk-in closet, seen overleaf, where clothes are folded onto open Perspex shelves and hung from Perspex hooks. A tall, narrow wooden unit houses towels and linens—all in regulation white. Another set of narrow wooden shutters, this time floor-length and painted, provide visual interest as well as complete privacy, and can be folded back to allow light to enter the room.

Part Three

Making it happen

getting started

The essence of simple style is paring down, avoiding unnecessary clutter, and creating an easy-to-live in, comfortable home environment. It isn't necessarily about minimalism, so don't feel you have to keep everything out of sight. Deciding on a specific look for your home will depend on personal taste, the existing property, your lifestyle, and the cost. An interior that reflects your own personality and passions is preferable to the sterility of a slavish dedication to a style.

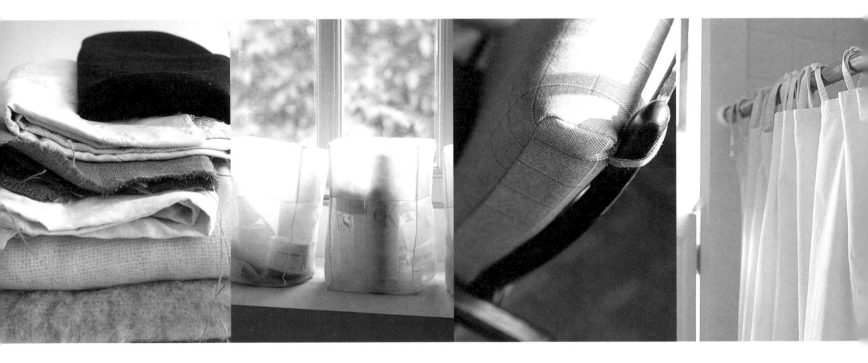

The selection of products and materials for domestic interiors has increased in the last few years. Many towns have stores and showrooms that offer a comprehensive range of kitchen and bathroom fixtures, flooring, heating, and lighting, as well as furniture and accessories. Antique shops and flea markets have also widened their scope to include newly fashionable retro items and many 20th-century design classics. Floors, walls, windows, fitted furniture, and fixtures form the shell of the interior, providing the essential backdrop for simple style. With the use of a restrained and consistent palette, an interior can be unified to create a feeling of space and harmony. Furnishings, essential equipment, and accessories, as well as your personal possessions, will enhance the space and add character. For ideas, look at books and magazines and visit showrooms, museums, and art galleries, but also take note of public and commercial buildings. Inspiration can come from unexpected sources—for instance, a color scheme can be based on a favorite painting or a collection of shells.

Stripping back

To provide the "blank canvas," or shell, on which to plan your interior, get back to the basic structural elements of floors, walls, and ceilings. Stripping out old or unattractive furnishings and fixtures will fully reveal the shape and structure of the space, highlighting previously unseen or unnoticed good features, as well as more negative aspects. Decide what can be disguised or ignored and what really needs changing. If you are fortunate enough to have large spaces, well-proportioned rooms, beautiful windows, and attractive architectural detailing, these features can be emphasized. If, on the other hand, your home is less distinguished, keep the interior simple, and make a statement with furniture and accessories.

Some properties may have been "improved" by the addition of poor-quality fixtures or the removal of original features, and this can be remedied. However, don't feel you have to be historically correct—taking away original moldings and detailing can enhance the inherent architecture. Also, don't be tempted to introduce "character" with old-style baseboards, architraves, and doors. Instead of imposing a particular style on the space, let the space dictate your decisions.

Floors should be unified, but can consist of different materials. If possible, take up all old floor coverings. The condition of the floor beneath will reveal any unsuitable surfaces. You may find original floor tiles, flagstones, parquet, or good-quality floorboards deemed unfashionable by the previous occupants. Such a lucky discovery could form the basis of the style, colors, and materials used elsewhere. If the floor is rough concrete or chipped tiles, consider floating a self-leveling topping over it to give a smooth surface, ready for the application of a new covering, such as stone, vinyl, or rubber tiles.

Walls can easily be redecorated, but a good surface is necessary. Strip away old wallpaper and wall coverings, and take off any unwanted tiles. If old tiles are in very good condition and unusual, they are worthy of repair and restoration.

Getting back to the bare plaster will ensure that such problems as cracks, damp patches, and rough finishes can be corrected. Wash and scrub the walls to remove traces of old paste, which might react with paint and cause discoloration. Lining paper covers flaws and gives a smooth base for paint, but imperfections are often characterful, particularly in older properties.

Paintwork on doors, window frames, architraves, and baseboards can usually be washed down with a commercial product and repainted. If the buildup of old paint masks the curves of moldings, you may need to use a paint stripper to reveal the detailing. Old paint may be lead-based, so it is best to leave it stable rather than sanding it down. Bare wood will need priming before painting; several new water-based, quick-drying products are available for this. Damaged paintwork can also be primed to produce a smooth, stable surface.

Fixtures can be replaced, but think carefully before taking out any piece that was included in the original interior; often these form part of the

all-white shell

contrasting textures

character of the building and are correctly proportioned.

Strip out any badly made or superfluous kitchen units, cabinets, and shelves. Consider replacing or removing unattractive doors, or using quality paneled versions. Boxed-in pipework sometimes spoils the clean lines of a room, so unless the casing forms part of the structure or the workmanship is of very high quality, remove it. Revealing the pipes may look better and create a more spacious feel, especially if they are painted the same color as the walls. If exposed pipes detract from the space, reroute them or conceal them within new structures.

Windows can be costly and impractical to change. Consider replacing frames if the old ones are in poor condition or not in the original style or material. Make sure that new windows are the correct style and proportion for your property—inappropriate window frames can have a detrimental effect on the price of your home. Since windows are part of the structure, consult an architect or building contractor before carrying out work.

Editing possessions

Unless you are starting from scratch or have a large budget, you will need to incorporate some existing furnishings and belongings into the available space. The simple-style approach involves creating a streamlined, pared-down environment, so be prepared to edit down your possessions.

Throw out or give away anything you don't need or like, or that doesn't work, is beyond repair, or is uncomfortable. Dispose of any inefficient or unwieldy storage units. Keep items you love, that are beautiful or full of character, and hold onto anything that is useful. Try to look at familiar items in a new way. Cleaning, repairing, repainting, or reupholstering can give new life to a piece.

Planning

Space, or the illusion of space, is an important aspect of simple style. The size and style of your home may impose certain limitations, but consider new ways of dividing up and using the space you already have. Knocking down interior walls or using floating partitions may seem attractive options; but think carefully before committing to an open-plan scheme—family life sometimes benefits from having small private areas for different activities. Consider what is going to work for you, as well as styles that inspire you. Don't get carried away with a visual idea without considering the practicalities first. Leaving the redesigning until after you move in will allow you to discover how sun positions, access paths, and your day-to-day needs influence the space, and may help you to avoid expensive mistakes. Using a scale plan of a room or of the whole area will enable you to see how the space can be reorganized and how the furniture fits into the plan. An architect can produce a detailed, technical plan, but you can make a simple drawing to help you see how your arrangements and ideas will work.

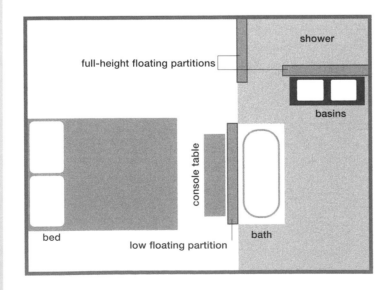

Left and above **In order to have a larger living space downstairs, a bedroom with an integral bathroom has been fitted into the opened-up attic. The floor of the bathroom area is raised to conceal the pipework beneath. A limestone tiled floor is used throughout.**

Floor plans

Measure a room carefully, and draw it on squared paper—the bigger the scale, the better. Draw in doors and their opening areas, and mark the positions of windows, radiators, outlets, closets, built-in cabinets, and light fixtures. Fit each room into a floor plan to build up a master plan.

Make templates of your main furniture, measuring at their widest points and using the same scale as the room drawing. Arrange them on your plan. Furniture often takes up a lot of space, and you will need to allow for outstretched legs on sofas and armchairs and enough room for pulling out, as well as sitting on, chairs around a table. Also allow space for opening closet and cabinet doors and drawers.

Assessing the space

Look at how best you can use and divide up the space, and experiment with ideas on your plan. Opening up the whole of one floor to create a large area for cooking, eating, and relaxing can work well. Simply removing doors can give a more open feel and easier access to living areas, though you will need to adhere to fire regulations. Consider unconventional ideas, such as "floating" partitions, using storage as a dividing wall, or placing furniture in the center of a room.

New stud partition walls can be easily constructed from a wooden or metal framework, covered with wallboard, plywood, or paneling, and then finished with plaster, paint, or veneer. For stability, a floating partition will need to be fixed at some point to the floor or ceiling.

It isn't always necessary to carry out extensive building works to substantially change how you use

space. Look at the way rooms are allocated and used. Traditionally, the kitchen and living spaces are downstairs and the bedrooms above, but upstairs rooms are often lighter and sunnier, with better views, so consider reversing the layout. Don't feel you have to finalize every detail—allow for a lucky find or a bright idea.

Professional advice

If you are considering structural alterations involving demolishing walls or enlarging openings, it is important to consult an expert first and get planning permission if necessary. Taking away structural walls requires a supporting beam to prevent the building, or parts of it, from falling down. An architect, structural engineer, or building surveyor will do the necessary calculations. When planning changes, it is worth employing an architect, as they offer innovative ideas as well as professional advice. Architects' fees normally include supervision of the building work, and they may recommend qualified building contractors.

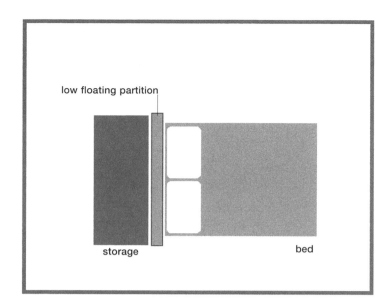

low floating partition

storage   bed

Left and below With the bed and clothes storage placed in the center of the room, on either side of a floating partition, this average-sized bedroom looks much more open and spacious.

Materials

Collect swatches, samples, and pictures of all the materials you are considering using, so that you can see how the colors and textures work together. Most stores and manufacturers will supply samples on request. Make a collage using the materials, as well as examples of your existing possessions. If you have a computer drawing program, you can quickly produce simple plans and scan in swatches and pictures of furniture. This can also be a good way to try out different colors and see how they change the mood and scale of a room.

Limiting the number of elements, materials, and colors will keep the interior looking simple and increase the feeling of spaciousness. Naturally finished woods and stone blend harmoniously, and when used with white or neutrals will provide a tranquil backdrop. Dark or highly polished surfaces, such as slate and marble, add accent and sophistication, but use them carefully and consistently. Flashes of color will brighten an environment, but for best results, use no more than two colors in a room. Make the most of different shades and tones of hues.

Surfaces

Materials for floors, worktops, walls, and fixtures are available in a comprehensive selection, including many products previously used commercially. Keep in mind how one room opens onto another, and choose surfaces that make a sympathetic transition.

Floor surfaces are available in a huge selection of wood and wood finishes, as well as stone and the increasingly popular concrete. Alternatively, there are vinyls, linoleum, rubber, and various carpetings, including sisal, coir, and sea grass, as well as wool.

Worktops in marble, slate, zinc, stainless steel, and concrete are frequently used, in addition to the ever-expanding range of solid woods and laminates.

Kitchen and bathroom fixtures, including sinks, basins, tubs, appliances, faucets, and lighting are widely available in a choice of different materials, colors, styles, and finishes. Even inexpensive ranges now offer stainless steel, colored enamels, and surfaces once considered purely at the luxury end of the market.

Furniture

Consider how your existing pieces will work with newer additions. Old and antique furniture often has attractive polished wood, stripped metal, or patinated surfaces. Matte-finished pale or dark woods, shiny- and satin-finish metal, plastics, and glass are prevalent in more modern furnishings. Leather looks warm and mellow when old, soft and sensuous when new.

Fabrics

Natural linens and cottons, soft wools, flannels, and felted wools are all ideal for a simple style approach. Faux furs and velvet add a tactile comfort. Using similar tones for all soft furnishings will maintain an understated look, whereas the addition of dramatic animal prints or colors can inject spirit and personality into a room.

Paints

Several paint ranges feature beautifully subtle shades and traditional-style finishes. Many of these paints tend to be denser and more matte than mass-market paints. Their characteristics are reflected in the colors, which tend to be more muted and similar in tone. As these edited ranges all share similar qualities, they naturally work well together. When used throughout an interior, they will create a unifying feel, even if the colors are quite different. Larger companies are now producing similar ranges, presented in various themes or moods, which makes choosing colors much easier.

harmonizing paint colors

Neutral palette

Neutrals are the colors of nature and harmonize well when used for surfaces and furnishing fabrics. They offer an infinite variety of tones and textures, from the dark intensity of granite gray to the mellow softness of creamy off-white and from coarse-weave linen fabrics to smooth felted wools.

White and denim blue

As timeless and comfortable as a much-loved and well-worn pair of jeans teamed with a crisp white shirt, denim and white will fit in with any style of interior. Denim fades and softens with use, so keep it in focus by combining it with fresh white paint. Blue-and-white stripes also add a touch of contrast.

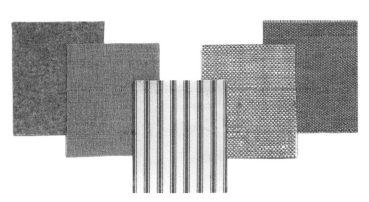

Red and white

Flashes of red add accent and definition to a predominantly white or neutral interior. Solid red should be used sparingly, but simple stripes and gingham checks, especially when used for curtains or bed linen, look cheerful and warm.

Floors

The desire for a more open, airy, and spacious feel in interiors has led to the resurgence of "bare" floors. The most frequently used material is wood, and a wide choice, from professionally laid, solid parquet to inexpensive laminates, is available. The natural properties of wood add character and warmth to a space. Limestone has become increasingly popular, as more varieties are now available and methods of laying less complex. Concrete, often a base for other forms of flooring, has become a valued material in its own right and is perfect for a modern look. Although these forms of flooring can be expensive, they are a permanent feature that, when properly installed, will add to the quality and value of your home. Since bare floors are part of the structure, rather than an added component, they contribute to the pared-down elemental ethos of the simple look.

Your choice will depend on budget, the existing floor, the suitability of the structure, and the position of your home. Take care to choose a reputable company—getting it wrong can be potentially disastrous, both structurally and financially. Remember, too, that bare floors are noisy. If you live in an upstairs apartment, your lease may stipulate that carpet must be laid for maximum sound insulation. A floor covering in a color or material that complements the interior can give a similar bare look and may be used successfully alongside wood, stone, or concrete.

parquet

laminates

floorboards

wood finishes

floors

Parquet

Traditional parquet floors are constructed from thick panels of wood, such as oak, birch, cherry, mahogany, or teak, often arranged in a basketweave pattern. New solid-block floors are expensive, but will last for many years and will improve with age.

Normally, parquet is installed over plywood or some other wood composite board. If it is to be laid over concrete, this should be dry and fully cured; if there is a risk of dampness, a protective layer of some kind, such as a dampproof membrane, should be used. In any case, the floor should be installed by a professional.

Less expensive, thinner varieties of parquet can be laid on top of existing floors. They are a viable alternative, provided they are installed correctly, though some have an unnatural, easy-care finish.

Old parquet floors can look dark and dull and may have loose or missing blocks, but repairing them is a worthwhile option. Treatments, such as sanding, oiling, and waxing, can also help to restore them to their former glory.

Laminates

Laminated wood floors are popular, as they are inexpensive and relatively easy to lay. The newer versions do not require gluing, but lock together and can be laid onto your existing floorboards. Ready-finished and usually stain-resistant, they are hard wearing and easy to maintain. Their composition varies; some incorporate real wood veneer, while others have a synthetic wood finish or metal effect. The composition should be stated on the store's label or the packaging.

It is important to do a little research on laminates before you buy. Laminate can swell and lift if subjected to contact with water; avoid using it in kitchens and bathrooms unless specified as suitable for these areas. The nonporous finish of some types of laminates can cause a buildup of condensation in the floor cavity below, with the consequent development of dry rot. Consult a professional or the manufacturer, if necessary.

Applying a liquid wax designed for laminates will help maintain a seal and minimize wear.

Floorboards

Wooden floorboards are the most common type of flooring, and existing boards in good condition are relatively easy to clean and treat. A variety of woods and widths are available, from inexpensive narrow pine boards, originally intended to be covered, to wide hardwood planks with attractive grains.

New floors can be laid using new or reclaimed wood. New wood has an even color, texture, and size, and is easy to work on. Usually, these are tongue-and-groove, and since there are no gaps between the boards, they make efficient and easy-to-clean flooring. Reclaimed wood is less consistent in size and quality, but has the advantage of an aged patina and inherent character. Reclaimed boards may require a considerable amount of preparation, both before and after laying, and extra is needed, as wastage can be up to 30 percent.

On original floorboards or reclaimed wood, sanding will remove dirt, old varnish, and paint, restore the character, and reveal the grain of the wood. Large gaps can be filled with strips of wood or

natural wood floorboards

parquet

pale oak floorboards

painted white floorboards

filler. Although replacing a damaged floorboard is fairly simple, if the overall condition is poor, a new floor should be installed, preferably by a professional. The techniques can be complex, and mistakes are difficult and costly to rectify. If you decide to lay a new floor yourself, do plenty of research first and discuss the job with an expert at your local lumberyard.

Wood finishes

All wood needs treating to protect the surface and prevent it from becoming dirty and discolored. Depending on the look you desire, the location, and the type of floor, you have a choice of oiling, waxing, bleaching, staining, and painting, as well as varnishes for sealing.

Most of the following treatments and finishes can be done yourself, but take time to research all of the available techniques and finishes first before deciding which to use. Some may be inappropriate for your existing materials and space, and can be difficult to remove if you do not like the result.

For all the processes, make sure you follow the health and safety recommendations for the materials you use. Wear protective gloves and a mask when using varnishes and paints, and make sure the whole house, as well as the room being worked on, is well ventilated. Always read the manufacturer's information on the container before buying to ensure that you get the correct product to suit the condition and composition of your floor.

Sanding wooden floors removes old varnish, wax, dirt, and minor imperfections, leaving a smooth, clean surface ready for treatment. Industrial sanders are available to rent, but it is always a dusty and messy business, so make careful preparations. Check there are no protruding nails or debris which might damage the sander. Make sure the room is well ventilated, and wear a mask to avoid breathing in the dust. Hanging a dampened drop cloth over the outside of the door will prevent some of the dust from escaping to other areas.

Varnishes and sealants are necessary for a hard-wearing surface, suitable for heavy use. A wide range of polyurethane varnishes and sealants are available in different colors and stains, and in matte and shiny finishes. These products can be used directly on new wood or on freshly sanded or cleaned wood. They can also seal stained or painted floors.

Efficiency and quick-drying properties are constantly being improved. However, speed isn't always everything, and sometimes the natural look is sacrificed in favor of ease of application. Even clear varnish will have an effect on the floor color, so test the varnish first in an inconspicuous area.

Waxing and oiling new wood prevents the wood from drying out and allows the floor to cope with day-to-day wear. Oil is the traditional treatment for wood flooring, with wax applied for further protection and to produce a mellow surface sheen.

Apply oil on new porous wood, so that it sinks into the surface. Oils such as teak and linseed will feed the floor, keeping it supple and scuff-free. Wax can be used as a finish itself or to preserve another finish. Apply the oil or wax with a brush or cloth, depending on the manufacturer's recommendations, but have cloths available to wipe away any surplus.

For a soft shine, wax can be buffed after application, using a lint-free cloth or a soft brush. Professional electric buffers can also be rented for large areas. Wax in liquid form is easiest to apply, and several commercial brands are available. Regularly oil and wax wood surfaces, especially on areas of heavy traffic and wear, to build up a self-protecting seal.

Staining floors brings out the grain and gives character to the wood, but will also highlight blemishes and imperfections. Wood stains are available in various finishes and colors. Dark stains and colors look dramatic, but they can make a room appear smaller.

Stains should be applied to a clean surface without any traces of old varnish or wax. They soak quickly into the wood and must be applied evenly to avoid a patchy effect. Be sure to do a small test in an inconspicuous area first, as color will vary depending on the existing wood; once applied, stains cannot be removed.

Bleaching gives a wonderfully pale, clean look to floorboards and also provides a soft surface that is kind to bare feet, which makes it particularly suitable for bedrooms. However, bleaching is not suitable for high-wear areas as bleached wood absorbs dirt easily.

The process requires a new or freshly sanded floor, and the bleaching technique must be commenced as soon as possible to prevent any orange tinge to the wood. Products used for this process consist of, or contain, oxalic acid. An oxalic acid powder can be mixed with water and mopped or sponged onto the floor, then rinsed off. A liquid form of bleach is also available.

An alternative to bleaching is a limed effect, in which the grain of the wood is emphasized by rubbing in a color, usually white. Liming wax is available from specialist paint

original stone

slate floor tiles

dealers, but you can get a similar effect by painting the floor with diluted latex flat paint and then rubbing down the surface with fine sandpaper to leave only the paint that has soaked into the grain. Seal with matte varnish to keep it clean.

Painting gives an overall flat finish and will cover imperfections in the wood surface. Specialized floor paint, available in a wide range of colors, has good covering properties and will produce a tough, robust surface which is easy to clean. An attractive worn look will develop in time, or the floor can be repainted if you prefer a new-looking effect. Painted floors can be slippery, especially in bathrooms, so make sure that any rugs or mats are secured with anti-slip devices.

For a soft, paint-washed look, use a water-based paint, such as latex flat. Water-based paints will soak into the wood and do not contain any plastics, which might

react adversely with the hardeners in varnish. Seal a painted floor with wax or varnish. Clear varnish applied on top of white paint tends to create a yellow tinge, so use floor paint for a pure white finish. Wax applied on top of a painted floor will give a mellow "aged" look, but will need regular applications to prevent the paint becoming dirty.

Stone

Stone is a beautiful and practical material. Derived from the earth, its inherent qualities and colorings bring a natural harmony to an interior. The soft, matte finish is part of the appeal of stone, but polished stone surfaces also have their own character and are a practical and sophisticated alternative.

Stone is unaffected by water (and flooding), which makes it particularly suitable for kitchens and bathrooms. It is, however, an unforgiving material—anything dropped onto it will probably break.

Also, as it does not absorb sound, it can be noisy, so think carefully before using it in a large area, especially where there are other hard flooring surfaces.

Old stone floors impart a sense of history to the homes in which they are found. Original flagstones may be uneven in texture and size, and their color varies according to the stone (usually local) used. New stone flooring is available in a wide variety of colorings, slab sizes, shapes, and finishes, from pale limestone to dark granite.

Because stone is quarried from the earth, its color, character, and properties will depend on geological factors. To the untrained eye, one piece of stone may look the same as another, but an expert will be able to distinguish good-quality stone from inferior. New stone is supplied in a variety of sizes, from standard tiles to slabs suited to large areas. Always consult, and buy your stone from, a recommended retailer.

Installing a new stone floor is best done by a professional. The veining and natural color variations that occur in some materials mean careful blending is required to give a natural-looking finish.

A level concrete base is normally necessary for laying stone, although it can also be laid onto a wood floor. The traditional method of laying slabs on a bed of sand and cement has mostly been replaced with the use of adhesives. Joints are grouted after laying, and for wood floors the adhesives and grout have flexible additives to allow for movement. Polished stone will normally be repolished after laying to provide a smooth, even surface.

Maintaining and caring for stone is easy. When stone is first quarried, it is relatively soft, but it starts to oxidize and become harder and less porous when exposed to air.

After laying, a stone surface is treated with a generous application of a silicon-based impregnator, which reduces the porosity. Regular washing with a neutral soap will feed as well as clean the stone. Matte finishes will develop a patina with use, but after approximately two years, oxidizing and constant walking over the surface will have encouraged the formation of a hard surface layer which is resistant to stains. At this point, the stone starts to "look after itself," needing very little cleaning and maintenance.

Limestone is currently popular for its pale, creamy tones, although grays, deeper colors, and speckled or randomly marked surfaces are also available. It is smooth to the touch and polished. One newly developed finish involves burning off the surface and polishing it with nylon brushes to leave raised areas that have smooth edges.

Slate has a natural distinctive "cleft" texture, which looks rugged and adds character to country-style properties and dramatic contrast to modern interiors. It can also be obtained with a smooth surface. Although available in different colors, including black, green, red, purple, and multicolors, the most sympathetic to a simple interior are the traditional grays, which range from charcoal to a whitish pale.

Marble is solidified limestone—it has turned to liquid in the earth before hardening again. It is usually

mosaic

associated with a distinctive pattern of veining, which can vary from the subtle blends of pale hues to more dramatic slashes of contrasting colors. Besides the familiar whites, grays, greens, and blues, there are warmer pinks and beiges.

Terrazzo

Terrazzo is formed of a mixture of marble aggregates, cements, and pigments which give it a distinctive speckly appearance. The enormous variety of finishes and colors is created by varying the size and color of the marble pieces as well as the amount of pigment.

The original method of applying terrazzo as a single slab, on site, created problems of shrinkage and cracking. Today, a more stable surface is achieved using precast and pre-polished tiles or units. As with stone, the tiles can be fixed with adhesive or by the more traditional method of setting tiles onto a bed of sand and cement.

concrete tiles

The terrazzo used in public buildings often has large pieces of aggregate in contrasting colors, but far more subtle finishes, which are more suited to domestic use, are also available.

Ceramic

Ceramic floor tiles are usually made from compressed porcelain fired to very high temperatures, which produces a hard-wearing, waterproof material with a consistent appearance. They are thicker and more robust than ceramic wall tiles. The shiny, glazed finish gives a clean, hard-edged look, especially when used with wall tiles in a similar color and finish (see page 190). Matte-finish tiles are now being produced in convincing imitations of stone, marble, and terrazzo, as well as a range of subtle finishes and solid colors.

Cheaper and less porous than stone, ceramic tiles are more consistent in size and color.

mosaic

concrete

linoleum

vinyl

rubber

natural

carpet

floors

Although they lack the character derived from the natural imperfections of stone, their evenness produces a smart, pristine look in a room.

For showers or areas where water is present, use a waterproof grout. If the surface beneath is flexible in any way, the grouted joints can pull away, allowing water to penetrate. The floor may need lengths of solid wood inserted between the joists to reduce movement and sheets of plywood fixed on top to ensure a level surface. If the consequences of water seepage are potentially catastrophic, incorporating a dampproof membrane into the construction is advisable.

painted concrete

polished concrete

Quarry tiles are a traditional form of ceramic tile with a dense, matte finish, usually in terracotta or dark brown, though they are also available in off-white. Old tiles have a pleasantly worn look, whereas new ones provide a flat, even-colored finish. Quarry tiles are normally laid onto a bed of mortar, but adhesives can be used. As with all tiles, a level concrete surface is best, but new adhesives and flexible additives in grout allow tiles to be laid onto other surfaces.

Mosaic

Mosaic tiles are small versions of ceramic tiles and are often used for more decorative work. Preformed mosaic, often in unsubtle colorings and inappropriate materials, has lessened in appeal. However, natural stone, ceramic, and glass mosaic tiles can be used to give a highly sophisticated and subtle look. Complicated patterns should be avoided, but a simple design

applied around the edge of flooring can be effective. Used in kitchens and bathrooms, stone and matte ceramic mosaics will have a natural appearance, and translucent glass looks elegant in bathrooms.

Concrete

Concrete forms the ideal base for many floor finishes, but it can also be used as a material on its own. It is especially appropriate for modern and industrial looks, but used boldly and confidently can look good in any interior, especially if installed throughout one level.

Whiteners are often added to cement, but pigments are also available to produce a variety of finishes, from a solid color to a more random effect. A polished finish, in which the concrete is floated level and then "polished" by repeated troweling, looks stunning and is highly practical.

Information on installing and finishing all types of concrete

projects is readily available from professional organizations. It is possible to carry out the work yourself, but seeking professional advice is recommended. The weight of the material makes it suitable for ground floors and basements only, unless the floor is reinforced, as in homes converted from industrial buildings. To support concrete slabs, the floor must be level, well-consolidated, and firm, so it won't move and settle, causing the concrete to crack. Several products are available to ensure that the concrete dries out properly, and expert advice should be sought, as it is important to use the right product at the right time.

The concrete can be sealed with an acrylic resin as soon as it has hardened, but most treatments are applied after 28 days. Once dry, the surface can be painted. Floor paint (see page 138) will cover well, but new products are constantly being developed.

Floor coverings

Replacing or installing new floors is not always possible for practical or cost reasons, and wood or hard floors may be too cold or noisy to suit your living arrangements. However, a dramatic change in the style of your home can be achieved with floor coverings, which may also add warmth and comfort. Solid-color coverings, used throughout a space, will link different areas and form a simple, unobtrusive background. Keep the look uncluttered by choosing one material that can be used in most of the rooms, adding softer surfaces, such as carpeting and rugs, where desired. If you decide to use more than one type of covering, choose complementary colors and finishes to maintain an impression of unified space. A number of floor finishes previously considered suitable for only kitchens and bathrooms, such as stone and concrete, are now popular in general living areas. Vinyl and rubber flooring, especially in tile form, can be successfully used for all rooms. The neutral tones and natural texture of sisal, coir, and sea grass matting is conducive to a calm ambience and can work in country-style settings, as well as more modern environments. Wall-to-wall carpet is quiet, warm, and comfortable, as well as cost-effective. Although generally unsuitable for kitchens or bathrooms, it can blend effectively with other floor finishes.

Linoleum

Linoleum is made from a mixture of natural materials, including wood flour, linseed oil, pigments, and natural resins, which give it a distinctive marbled pattern. Used extensively from Victorian times to the mid-1900s, it then went out of fashion as newer materials became available and wall-to-wall carpet was more affordable. In more recent years, linoleum has become popular in multicolored floor designs; these are produced by a large number of specialist manufacturers.

Appreciated for its natural ingredients, subtle coloring, and matte finish, linoleum looks best in a single color. Careful laying, using adhesive, on a smooth, sound surface is required, and this is best accomplished by a professional.

Vinyl

Vinyl is often thought of as a less expensive and more hard-wearing form of linoleum, and certain types are now considered unfashionable. It is easy to clean and cool underfoot. Inexpensive varieties are available in sheet form and need no adhesive. The available designs tend to be a little complicated, but plain terrazzo-effect and checkerboard patterns are simple and neutral enough to work well. More expensive and sophisticated vinyl floorings are available in a selection of colors, patterns, and finishes, including imitations of terracotta, stone, and wood. If a simple design is chosen, vinyl can be used to stunning effect.

Vinyl needs to be laid onto a completely flat and even surface, such as a self-levelling topping or a layer of hardboard, so that the imperfections or texture of the floor beneath do not show or cause wear. Neat cutting and laying is necessary to avoid badly fitting edges, creases, and buckling. Avoid vinyl for large areas, as unsightly joins may be needed. In these cases, choose vinyl tiles, which can be fixed with adhesive.

Rubber

Rubber is warm, practical, and good for sound insulation. Widely used in schools, hospitals, and athletic clubs, it is robust, with a fashionably matte finish. The range of solid colors makes it popular for domestic use; however, it can be expensive. Although a number of treatments to seal the surface are available, rubber will mark easily. Blemishes and indentations may not show up in a large commercial building, but may be more noticeable in a domestic setting.

Natural coverings

This form of floor covering, which includes sisal, coir, sea grass, and jute, is the natural alternative to traditional carpeting. All varieties are spun from plant fiber. The appeal of these materials is their distinctive textures. Their natural appearance and neutral coloring make them ideal for a simple approach, as they blend with wood and gently contrast with pale walls.

These coverings are woven in a variety of patterns, from flat weaves to bolder herringbones, and some types feature colorful stripes or borders. In addition to a range of widths for fitting wall-to-wall, there are also area rugs, which can be edged with cotton tape, leather, suede, or felt.

Although hard wearing, the coarse textures can be unfriendly to bare feet, especially for young children. However, finer and tighter weaves are smoother, and some coir and sea grass have a softer feel. Versions using wool, linen, cotton, and other smoother fibers have recently become available.

Maintenance can be a problem with these coverings, as dirt is not easily removed, and accidental spills can stick between the fibers. Many woven coverings are pre-treated with a stain-resistant finish, and newer weaves and treatments make them less prone to dirt. Some sisal rugs are reversible and can be turned over when one side is dirty. Being a natural product, the floor coverings will wear and mature in an attractive way.

Carpet

Bare floors can be cold and noisy, and carpeting provides quiet luxury at a price that is often far below other floor treatments. Carpet can also add a touch of warmth to hard floor surfaces or announce a change of setting in a space.

There is an enormous choice of fibers and weaves in carpeting. Although wool is warm and luxurious, it is relatively expensive. The most popular fiber is nylon, which is sometimes combined with wool. Carpet pile can be finished in a variety of textures—cut (plush or twisted), loop (either level or multi-level), and a combination of the two.

A subtle texture in neutral and soft natural colors, including beiges and grays, are the best choices for a simple look. Dark colors make rooms appear smaller and will also show dust and fluff, but can introduce a change of mood or a touch of drama in spacious homes.

Walls

Plain, pale walls and paintwork will enhance the feeling of space and provide a smooth backdrop for more textured furnishings. Using the same color or tones throughout keeps the look simple and unifies a collection of small rooms. Although white or off-white walls are the favored choice, they are not compulsory. Subtle tints, bold hues, and careful use of wallpaper, paint effects, or stenciling can provide an accent, focus, or a change of mood in an interior. Bare walls create a serene, uncluttered impression and allow other features, such as architectural detailing, materials, and furnishings, to stand out. Light also reflects better off plain walls.

A good surface is necessary for the application and finished appearance of paint. With large areas of plain wall, any imperfections will show, so repair cracked surfaces with filler or consider replastering or skimming. Some interiors, such as country properties, may have rough-plastered walls or original wood beams, which enhance and complement the structure, and these should be retained, if possible. Doors, baseboards, window frames, and picture and chair rails are normally decorated in a more hard-wearing alkyd-based paint. To minimize the effect of paint fumes, increase the drying times; water-based paints have been developed in eggshell and satin finishes, as well as gloss, which make application easier and cut down on fumes.

surfaces

paint types

paint colors

stenciling

wallpaper

walls

Surfaces

Whatever your wall surface, the effect will be simplest if most of the walls are treated in the same way. That doesn't mean color, texture, or materials are forbidden. Plain plaster walls will blend, exposed brick looks dramatic, and paneling adds elegance.

Plaster covered with smooth paint is the surface most people opt for. Rough, damaged, or textured walls can be skimmed with a thin coat of plaster by a professional to give an even surface. The true character of stone-built properties will be retained if the walls are of rough-rendered, unrestored plaster, particularly those revealing an attractive patinated or painted finish, which can be sealed with a matte acrylic varnish for cleaning.

Tiles are eminently practical in kitchens and bathrooms, where they provide a waterproof, easy-clean surface. Ceramic tiles are available in an ever-widening range of finishes, including stone and slate, and stainless-steel tiles can also be found (see pages 138–9).

Paneling is usually part of the original architecture and helps to form the character of a house. In a simple interior, the detailing will stand out without the need to highlight it in a different color. If a wall is uneven, or there is a noise or damp problem, installing plain paneling can be a solution.

Tongue-and-groove gives a country-style feel and is useful for covering up an uneven or unsightly wall finish. It is readily available from home centers in 3 1/2- and 5-inch (9- and 13-cm) widths, but can be custom-cut if desired.

"Raw finishes", such as exposed brick, concrete, and bare plaster, are simple and fashionable. They are, however, prone to dust and they will need sealing. Several commercial products give a clear invisible coating, but get advice, as some sealants result in an unnatural, shiny appearance.

Paint types

Each of the different paint ranges on the market has its own specific look and suitability for use. Generally, latex paints are used for walls and are essentially water-based. Gloss and eggshell finishes are applied to woodwork and are frequently alkyd-based, though water-based versions are now available. Specialist companies have also adapted the content of their paints to minimize any detrimental effects on the environment and health.

Latex flat paint is a standard finish for walls. It is an easy-to-apply water-based paint, available in a huge range of colors, many of which can be mixed to your precise specifications. Modern latex paints cover well, sometimes with just one coat, and can be wiped clean. They can be applied to most cleaned and prepared sound surfaces, including bare plaster, wallpaper, old paint, brick, stone, and wood. Spray painting is a useful method for covering textured surfaces.

Buttermilk paints have been developed due to the recent revival of interest in some of the homemade paints of earlier times. Some of these used skim milk, which was allowed to curdle and was then mixed with natural pigments. Modern buttermilk paints are made from more stable ingredients, but they reproduce the appealing natural colors characteristic of 18th- and 19th-century America. The paints can be used on walls (with a suitable primer) and woodwork, and they dry to a soft, matte finish. For greater opacity, apply more coats; for a translucent, stain effect, mix the paint with water.

Simulated whitewash is an acrylic-latex paint that replicates the look of traditional whitewash, but it s much easier to apply. It is suitable for exterior, as well as interior, walls and can be colored with tints.

Trim paints create a hard-wearing coating that preserves and protects wood surfaces. Windows, door frames, and baseboards are susceptible to scuffing and finger marks, and window frames are vulnerable to condensation. Traditionally, alkyd- and oil-based gloss paints have been used, as they form a hard, water-resistant coating, but they are also difficult to apply, and care must be taken to produce a smooth surface.

Water-based versions, including gloss, eggshell, and some new flat finishes, have been developed, and these are safer for the environment and your own health. Gloss trim paint looks fresh and clean, reflects the light, and highlights woodwork. Eggshell has a soft sheen which creates a more subtle look. The new flat finishes are low-sheen or matte, which enables them to blend with the

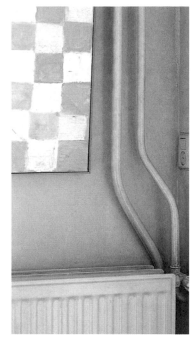

latex flat paint

wallpaper

gloss trim paint

walls and gives a wonderfully restrained look to a room, but they are not recommended for kitchens or bathrooms.

Paint colors

An interest in "heritage" styles, along with the demand for ever-more subtle finishes, has led to a number of specialist paint companies' developing ranges that reproduce the shades and softer finishes of past eras. Collections made for major paint companies by well-known designers are also available. These tend to focus on the latest trends and often include useful categories, such as whites and neutrals. Many of the large paint companies have redefined their color choices and offer ranges that are based on moods, as well as historical and architectural styles.

Wherever you buy your paint, you will already be aware that white is no longer just white. There

are numerous versions, from the blue brightness of "brilliant" white to the greige tints of lime-white. Brilliant white is the most inexpensive and it dominates the shelves of large home centers. Because it contains blue, it can look cold and harsh, and may also be unflattering to the space and its contents. It is a little unforgiving, too, as it highlights imperfections and can make perfectly clean items look dirty.

Look for plain white, which is softer-looking and not as expensive as special blended whites. It can often be found at home centers in contractor grade (which tends to be slightly thicker for better coverage but does not wear as well).

Neutrals include the darker shades of white as well as soft tones of gray, beige, gray-green, and light brown, which correspond to the colors of wood, stone, natural fibers, and pale foliage.

Stenciling

Although considered a more ornate form of wall decoration, stenciling can also be used in a restrained, simple way. Limiting the palette can ensure continuity throughout a home, while introducing a subtle pattern as variation. As with paint effects, use colors that are similar in tone or character. Some of the historic paint collections share a similar quality even when the colors are quite different, and will all work well together.

Wallpaper

Wallpaper is back in fashion, but the modern approach is to use it in a more limited way. Apply a decorative wallpaper on just one wall for use as a feature, or use it in a small room where the rest of the contents are low key or similar in style, color, or material. The newest ranges of wallpaper combine large-scale patterns with more subtle colorings.

Windows

Plain, uncomplicated curtains, draperies, blinds, shades, or shutters, or no window coverings at all, are an important feature of a simple-looking interior. Ornate headings and valances have been replaced by plain poles, rods, wires, and ungathered curtains, hung on metal curtain rings, threaded through large grommets, or attached to clip-on rings. If you are fortunate enough to have beautiful, well-proportioned windows, and the benefit of privacy and a pleasant view, you can leave the windows unadorned. Alternatively, shutters, blinds, simple panels, or plain curtains can cover or disguise unsightly windows and minimize their impact. Small window proportions can be altered in emphasis by using full-length curtains, translucent panels, or shutters to give the illusion of height. Lined draperies may be vital to keep out drafts and, in towns, to filter the dust and grime of city streets. Window coverings filter and regulate the light, which can substantially change the mood of a space. Consider the aspect and function of the room; for example, covered windows at night give a warmer, more intimate feel.

curtains/ draperies

hardware

shades/blinds

Curtains/draperies

Various fabrics and lengths of curtain or drapery can be used in an interior, depending on your lighting and draft-proofing requirements, as well as the proportions and style of the space. Experiment with a sheet draped over a pole to see how different lengths work with your window and space proportions. Hemming curtains midway between the windowsill and the floor gives a "floating" effect, which works particularly well with high ceilings.

An interior that responds to seasonal changes allows for the welcome light of spring and summer, and the chillier fall and winter evenings. In the winter months, heavier draperies can be substituted for lightweight versions. Long panels in heavy felted wool which skim the floor will form an efficient draft excluder.

While heavier weights of fabric, such as wool or flannel, add warmth, lightweight voile, muslin, plain cottons, and linens create a fresh summery feel. Solid colors allow the fabric to blend in with the walls, but this is not the only option—a pale damask or burlap fabric can bring a little textural relief in an otherwise stark space.

Panels are the simplest form of window covering. Hemmed lengths of ungathered fabric can be fixed at the top with ties, tabs, grommets, or rings, or threaded onto a slim pole or wire through a casing. Wide panels can be treated as simple draperies, pulled back to each side when more light is required. Translucent panels, either alone or combined with heavier draperies, make an ideal permanent covering by allowing light diffusion and extra privacy.

Panels are easy to make, but most home-decorating stores and departments now sell an excellent range of ready-made versions.

Ready-made draperies in solid-colored fabric are extremely good value. Many are made with tabbed tops, ties, simple casings, or grommets. Others have traditional pleat-tape headings, designed for use with hooks, but these can be used ungathered and hung from rings on less conventional hardware, such as tension wire or a galvanized metal rod.

Double draperies provide additional insulation during the cold months of the year. Instead of changing the draperies at the

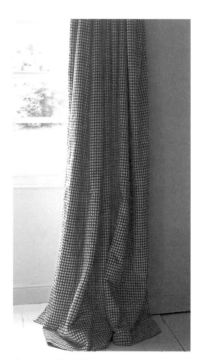

long padded drapery

onset of colder weather, simply add a thicker panel behind the summer covering, using a length of Velcro to secure it. This method provides a cleaner look than a double traverse rod system and maintains the style of the more lightweight fabric.

Padded draperies are another option for conserving heat during colder seasons. Padding lightweight fabric with batting can keep out drafts. Batting in varying thicknesses can be inserted between two fabric layers to create a reversible padded drapery.

Hardware

Plain metal rods or wires create a streamlined effect that looks stylish when paired with drapery panels in unlined plain fabrics. However, there are many other types of hardware that can blend into the walls or be concealed. Avoid complicated traverse rod systems, as they can look obvious and overbearing in a simple interior. Heavy weights of fabric can be hung on conventional traverse rods or on simple metal poles.

More decorative fixtures, such as clip-on rings or poles in modern styles, can be used as a feature. These work best if they link with other hardware in the space; for example, by using aluminum fixtures in a room where the door handles and furniture legs are also aluminum.

Curtain and drapery hardware is constantly being improved to facilitate new decorating styles. For example, you can now buy a traverse rod designed for tab-top draperies—thus combining the simplicity of this style with the convenience of being able to open and close the draperies without pulling on the fabric.

Buying all the hardware separately is often possible, and because the sizes tend to be standard, you can mix and match them. Using wooden poles with simple metal hardware and rings will look lighter and fresher than wood or imitation wood rings.

Rods in a range of metal finishes, most with shaped finials, can be bought in department stores and home centers. Chain stores now have excellent ranges of rods, simple finials, and rings in stainless steel, as well as in galvanized and dull metal finishes.

Lengths of metal rod, including galvanized piping, used as reinforcing rods or for plumbing, can be found in building materials dealers and home centers. Buying this way not only is cheaper, but also avoids the extra cost of unwanted decorative finials and brackets, which are often included in ready-packaged systems. In addition, the brackets and fixings for pipework is plain, practical, and simple. Steel engineering rods, available from architectural and hardware wholesalers, have an attractive, minimalist look.

Wooden poles are a good alternative, but buy them without finials on the ends. If you own thick, old-fashioned wooden poles, these can be easily painted to merge with the background.

Curtain wire systems were initially devised using techniques and materials available in hardware shops and builders' suppliers. Now available from home centers and chain stores, they have been adapted for ease of use, and they look more sophisticated, often containing stainless-steel components. As with metal and traverse rods, these systems include all necessary hardware.

Curtain rings can look clean and simple when sewn onto flat drapery panels. Look for fine iron and steel, rather than brass or old-fashioned wood rings, and thread the rings onto slim metal rods.

clip-on rings

grommets

Several variations on curtain rings now exist, including metal rings with a loop for hooks.

Clip-on rings have a metal attachment that clips onto the curtain fabric without the need for tape or hooks. They can be bought in plain or decorative styles in a range of different finishes. Choose lightweight versions for thinner voile or muslin fabrics and more robust clips for heavier cottons and linens.

Grommets, or eyelets, are a neat and streamlined way of hanging curtains, as they eliminate the need for hooks or rings and enable the curtain to slide effortlessly over the rod. Large versions are available for hanging heavier weights of fabric. Grommets work well on close weaves of fabric, such as linen, thick cotton, or felted wool. Try to match the grommet finish to the rod finish

and make sure that the grommet used is the correct size for the rod.

Grommets are usually sold in kits, which include the tools for cutting and securing them. Space according to the weight of fabric—heavier curtains will require more closely spaced eyelets. Do not insert the grommets too near the top edge of the panel, as the weight of the fabric may cause it to pull away from the eyelets.

Shades/blinds

Shades and blinds maintain a clean look, whether they are efficient venetian blinds or soft, gauze Roman shades. Shades use a minimal amount of fabric and can be drawn up into simple pleats. Because shades and blinds are usually fitted to the size of the window, and hung within the recess, they leave the walls free and can lighten the feel of a room. When constructed in a material that matches the walls, they will blend into the background when closed. They can be used to disguise less attractive windows or serve as a discreet presence on beautiful ones.

Shades and blinds are adaptable; they can filter the light or even block it out, providing subtle light control as well as forming a convenient screen. Many types are available ready-made. Wood, metal, paper, fiber, bamboo, reed, and plastic, as well as fabric, complement different interior styles and can be chosen to suit the function of the space.

Roller shades are the neatest and plainest form of shade. They can look formal in stiffened fabric and almost invisible when made from muslin. Rolled up, roller shades are barely noticeable and will not interfere with the light or impinge on an uncluttered space. They look best when secured to the inside of a window frame, but blinds can also be hung over the top of the window if necessary.

Ready-made roller shades, including blackout and water-resistant versions, can be bought in various widths and may be cut to fit. They are normally available in white or cream. Roller shades can also be custom made, using any suitable fabric of your choice, coated with vinyl for stiffening.

A recent development is paper roller shades, which look fresh and modern. The surface of the paper has small cut-outs, which add texture and create interesting light and shadow effects.

Roman shades lie flat against the window when lowered and form neat pleats when pulled up with

woolen Roman shade

translucent linen Roman shade

cords, threaded through rings on the back. For a crisp effect, the rings are sewn to narrow pockets containing dowels; dispensing with the pockets and dowels produces a softer, informal style.

Thick cotton or natural linen are ideal choices of fabric. Lightweight translucent fabrics will filter the light and are good in summer or for spaces that don't need to be draft-proof or light-proof. Shades that are slightly wider and longer than the windows can be cozy and efficient, especially if made in heavier fabrics, such as woolen flannel or lined cotton. They can be lined with blackout lining or insulating fabric.

Although Roman shades—especially the more unstructured styles—are relatively simple to make, ready-made versions are available in a variety of widths, lengths, and materials. To maintain a simple look, avoid scalloped or other decorative edges.

Venetian blinds once were expensive, often had to be made to measure, and were considered difficult to keep clean. Their hard-edged look came to be associated more with offices than with domestic interiors. However, they are now appreciated for their clean lines, which complement modern spaces and warehouse-style lofts.

Wood looks softer and warmer than metal blinds and will blend with most interiors. Dark wood can be dramatic, but may look heavy if used in small spaces or on small windows. Pale or paint-washed wood will be less dominant and will allow more light to enter the room. The thickness and depth of slats varies; choose thinner, narrower versions for a more subtle look. Because some of the blind will always be seen, consider where you place it. For example, venetian blinds would not be appropriate or practical on French doors which open into the room.

fabric shutters

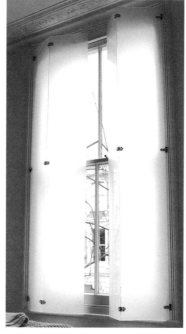

Perspex shutters

Wooden blinds look better if they are left down permanently, providing a gentle form of light control when open and an efficient blackout at night.

Metal venetian blinds can have very thin and narrow slats, which make them less conspicuous than wood. Available to order in a large range of colors, they are widely available in standard widths in white and silver. They look cool and sophisticated, especially when incorporated into the design of the interior, but can appear cold and clinical, if used with lots of hard edges and expanses of white. Metal blinds can be highly effective on picture windows, where they can be adjusted to open up or close off a view.

Natural fiber shades and blinds, made from such materials as reed, bamboo, and paper, are inexpensive and add a definite textural effect. Their simple

structure and mechanisms often make them easy to cut to the correct width.

Used as a permanent window covering, they soften the look of an interior and can screen any unattractive views. The different materials vary in their translucency; although all will provide a degree of privacy during daylight, some become transparent when the lights are on at night. Pleated paper and fiber shades are usually fairly opaque, but may look a little heavy, if left down during the day.

Shutters

Interior shutters can complement or emphasize beautiful, well-proportioned windows and disguise or cover up less attractive styles. The versions that fold away completely allow tall, elegant windows to be displayed. Double shutters are particularly useful as the top section can be left open to let in light, while the bottom serves

as a screen for privacy. An illusion of a floor-length window can be created by placing full-length double shutters across an ordinary window and opening just the top.

Traditionally, shutters fit inside the window frame, but if your frames are metal or fit flush with the wall, or you wish to cover the whole window, the shutters can be fixed outside the frame. Not all windows are suitable for shutters. Check the frame to work out where hinges can be attached and to see if there is space for folding back the shutters. Take care to work out every aspect of how the shutter will open and close.

To ensure that the shutter can be moved through 180 degrees, strips or small blocks of wood may need to be fixed to the wall so that the hinges are level with the frame edge. Double hinges will enable panels to fold back on themselves. The shutter manufacturer or retailer will recommend the best hinge for your window.

Wood, naturally finished or painted, is the most frequently used material, and this is normally used to make the familiar louvered shutters. Other materials include plywood and medium-density fiberboard (MDF)—although these will, of course, shut out light completely. For more sophisticated designs involving panels, or for a home that is architecturally distinctive, employ a professional carpenter to custom-make and install the shutters.

Translucent acrylic sheet, such as Perspex, filters the light beautifully and looks modern, yet delicate. A relatively expensive material, acrylic

needs to be cut carefully to avoid cracking, and the edges must be smoothed down without damaging the surface. Acrylic scratches easily, so avoid using it in areas where it may be subjected to rough treatment. You will need extra sets of hinges to ensure that this slightly flexible material will not warp. Unless you can buy ready-finished pieces, it is best to have them professionally made.

Lightweight fabric may be hung on a narrow frame or slender metal rods, as seen far left, and secured with simple screw hooks or eyes. It combines the practicality and visual impact of a shutter with the translucence of muslin or gauze.

Screens

Using screens in front of a window can provide privacy while leaving the windows bare and uncluttered. They may be easily moved, or removed, to suit different times of day or changing seasons. The newest versions are made from translucent materials, including paper, gauze, and acrylic sheet. Paper screens in a wooden frame give a crisp feel to a room. The traditional wooden folding screen is flexible and adaptable, but there are also sculptural, curved shapes available in slatted wood, lightweight plastics, and paper of varying thicknesses.

Simple screens can be made from lengths of wood or medium-density fiberboard (MDF), joined with hinges. Old screens may be found in junk shops and antique markets. Look for old hospital-style screens on wheels, which can easily be rejuvenated with a coat of paint and some new fabric.

Heating

The type of heating you choose depends on where you live and what is available and practical for your home. Warm air and under-floor (also called in-floor) heating systems are the least intrusive methods, leaving you free to place furniture and fixtures without too many restrictions. They are usually installed when the house is built, but can be incorporated into new building works. It is worth considering installing an under-floor system if you are having a new floor laid; a concrete or wood floor works particularly well with this form of heating.

If you live in an older house or apartment, your heating system may incorporate radiators, which can be unsightly and must be dealt with in some way when planning the design of your interior. There are various ways of disguising or concealing radiators; alternatively, you can replace old ones with visually pleasing ones. Conversely, you may be fortunate in having one or more fireplaces in your home, whether they are original period pieces, reproductions, or modern inserts, and they can serve as welcoming, warming focal points, with or without a real fire burning. Stoves, whether inherited with the home or newly installed, are similarly comforting and can also be a source of heating. Their shape and size can turn them into a sculptural presence or part of the architecture of the space. Before undertaking any renovation of a fireplace or stove, or using one for the first time, consult a chimney sweep or home-heating expert, who can make the necessary safety checks.

radiators

fireplaces

gas fireplaces

stoves

tall modern radiators

cast-iron radiators

industrial radiators

Radiators

Modern radiators are attractive and an efficient method of heating. Smaller sizes can now heat larger spaces, while requiring less wall space. The variety of types and choice of materials and colors are such that it is possible to find designs that suit the style and character of any property. Making radiators as discreet as possible has always been paramount, but the availability of new shapes and finishes offers the chance to use them as a feature. Plain, flat panels or radiator covers, painted in the same color as the wall, will be barely noticeable. Placing tall, slim radiators behind doors maximizes otherwise unusable space and keeps the rest of the wall clear. Low, floor-level radiators also have minimal impact.

Old-fashioned cast-iron radiators, found in old houses, schools, and office buildings, are currently popular. Their generous proportions and industrial style are well suited to large rooms, lofts, warehouse-style dwellings, and older properties. Reconditioned old radiators can be found in architectural salvage yards, and several manufacturers have now added retro styles to their ranges.

Modern and distinctive designs are produced by specialized radiator manufacturers. Dramatic spirals, curves, and grids, from long and low shapes to tall and slim, can be used in selected areas, such as bathrooms, where they give the space a certain distinction. Because they possess such a dramatic presence, use them as a single feature in an otherwise minimal space.

minimal fireplace

traditional fireplace

Fireplaces

If you wish to open up and use a previously boarded-up fireplace, note that there are strict rules and regulations in some areas relating to pollution and health and safety. Before carrying out any changes, consult a chimney sweep, building contractor, or heating expert, and check with your local government on any possible restrictions on the use of fuel. A good chimney sweep can advise you on the state and efficiency of your chimney, and will be able to point out any possible negative consequences of changes you wish to make.

A newly opened-up fireplace with an exposed firebox and hearth looks attractive, and it may be possible to use it in this raw state. However, the chimney can be damaged if the old bricks are not sound, so consult an expert for advice. A raised hearth may be constructed using bricks, but the shape and construction of the chimney can limit where you place

the fire. You may wish to adapt, change the style, or raise the level to create a fireplace without a mantelpiece or hearth to spoil the minimal lines, see above left.

Another option is to have a mason build a fireplace in your home, but this is an expensive process. A more economical method is to install a wood-burning insert into existing masonry.

Mantels and fire surrounds come in a great variety of styles, including Colonial, Victorian, and modern designs. If you dislike the existing surround, you can replace it with another. However, the grate may be sealed to the fireback with asbestos, a hazardous material that must be handled and disposed of by a professional.

Traditional fire surrounds and mantelpieces with graceful curves and proportions will enhance many styles of interior, especially if they do not have any ornate detailing

or tiles. Architectural salvage companies and antique shops stock a variety of fire surrounds in different shapes and sizes and in marble, stone, wood, and metal. Specialist companies sell both reconditioned and new mantels and fire surrounds, some in attractive, plain styles. Alternatively, a carpenter can build you a simple shape in wood, which can then be painted or otherwise finished.

Gas fireplaces

If you have a fireplace and would like to use it for heating, but wish to avoid the dust and mess inevitable with a real fire, you might consider installing a gas fireplace. Modern versions that replicate log or coal fires can be convincing, without being ornate or artificial-looking. Several new, innovative designs include simple stone bowls filled with flaming pebbles and dramatic sculptural shapes incorporating real flames. For these

types, a chimney is needed, and a flue liner may be required to avoid the buildup of harmful gases.

Stringent regulations apply to gas-fueled fires. Make sure that the fireplace you buy meets the standards of the American Gas Association and that it is installed by a state-licensed contractor.

Stoves

Wood-burning and other solid-fuel stoves are efficient sources of heat and some can also heat water. Clean and contained, they have the feel of a real fire, but are much safer. Their simple, ergonomic shapes can look stylish, especially in matte black or stainless-steel finishes. Scandinavian stoves are sought after for their modern and well-designed appearance.

In the absence of a chimney, connecting stoves to a balanced flue placed on an outside wall may be possible, but you will need expert advice and installation.

Lighting

Lighting has an enormous influence on an interior and can completely change the ambience of a space, from bright efficiency to subdued intimacy or anything in between. It is a huge area, with a wide choice of styles and categories suited to specific purposes and levels of illumination. Start with good, general lighting, then use individual lamps to create different moods and highlight specific areas or objects. Floor-standing, table, and desk lights can be moved, so changing their effect is easily achieved. Installing dimmer switches allow the light intensity to be precisely adjusted. Simple lighting solutions can mix the practical, sophisticated, and understated, while also injecting occasional touches of flamboyance and romanticism.

The industrial look, with its honest use of materials and simple construction, is perfect for large spaces and pared-down interiors. Work lamps, especially the clip-on variety, are adaptable and usually inexpensive, and the angled desk lamp can be used in many locations unconnected with work. Old light fixtures rescued from factories and offices may be found in salvage yards, antique shops, and even dumpsters and junkyards. An unusual table lamp can inject character into a minimal space or become a striking stand-alone feature. Large ranges of modern, beautifully designed lamps, light fittings, and complete systems may be found in interior-decorating stores, as well as specialist retailers, some of which also stock classic 20th-century designs. The increased demand for good, modern style means that even chain stores offer suitable contemporary lighting, often at remarkably low prices.

overhead

concealed

wall

work

table and floor

lighting

Overhead lighting

General overhead lighting, fixed to the ceiling, is used for areas where high light levels are required, such as kitchens, bathrooms, work spaces, and staircases. A single central light is now considered unfashionable, as it casts a harsh light over the whole area, but fitting dimmer switches will enable greater light control.

Downlighters, normally set into the ceiling, will give good general light, and this unobtrusive form has replaced tracks of spotlights as the favored light source in kitchens. Setting them near the edges of a room, so that the light "washes" down the wall, produces a more subtle effect. Downlighters are somewhat complicated to fit since they need to be set into the ceiling; consequently, they may be unsuitable for certain properties.

Overhead spotlights throw good directional light onto working areas and can be angled upward for a wash of light. Long tracks with several spotlights are not as fashionable as they once were, but smaller groups of up to four bulbs, fixed onto a short track or central round plate, are now available in a whole range of styles and finishes, including white, aluminum, stainless steel, and brushed steel.

Independent shaped bulbs or spotlights can look stylish when hung on long cables, either singly or in rows. The bulbs may be moved along the cable to suit your requirements. They look good in both modern and old properties.

A number of beautifully designed, highly sophisticated spotlight systems can also be purchased. Normally specified by architects and interior designers, they involve tracking systems and offer high levels of light control. They are more costly and will need professional installation.

Hanging, or pendant, lamps are set low to throw a pool of concentrated, more controlled, light over an area. There are no fixed rules for their height—it depends on the style and function of the piece. Some versions have a rise-and-fall mechanism, so that the height can easily be adjusted. However, if you are using a hanging lamp over a table, make sure that the bulb won't shine uncomfortably into your eyes when you are seated, and that you will not bang your head when sitting down or reaching for food.

Glass, plastic, and paper shades will diffuse the light, as well as direct it, whereas metal or other opaque materials throw all the light downward. Large utilitarian aluminum shades are a good choice for simple, spacious rooms.

Chandeliers can lend a little frivolity to sparse settings. A simple interior need not be a severe one, and an unashamedly pretty chandelier can serve as an elegant focal point. Sculptural or modern forms will introduce curved shapes to a hard-edged interior, traditional delicate crystal versions look romantic, and unique quirky finds can add character.

naked bulb in a ceramic outlet

work lamp

pendant light

angled desk lamp

Concealed lighting

With concealed lighting, there are no visible fixtures and fittings to spoil the clean lines of an interior. The light source is normally set behind discreet panels at ceiling or floor height, but sophisticated versions are incorporated into the interior design at the planning stage. Concealed lighting can be created by installing a panel in front of a row of downlighters, spotlights, or a striplight, but check the safety recommendations to ensure that the panel does not become a fire hazard.

Concealed lights beneath kitchen units provide good worktop lighting without illuminating the whole space. They are usually incorporated into the kitchen design and installed, along with the units, but simple plug-in versions can be bought to fit under cabinets or shelves.

A variety of recessed and concealed lighting has been designed for bathroom use, and many systems include mirror lights. When installing lighting in a bathroom, check that the fixture is certified by the UL as suitable for "damp" locations. It is best to have the work done by a professional.

Wall lights

Wall lights give a soft form of light and are frequently used in kitchens and bathrooms, where they are functional rather than decorative. When used above countertops, sinks, and basins, they are neat and understated, but give out plenty of diffused light. The plainest types are circular ceramic lights that can be attached to the wall. Bulkhead lights are contained, waterproof units which may be used outdoors and in bathrooms. With their wire protective covering, they look functional, but more sophisticated versions feature etched glass with narrow, stainless-steel rims.

Work lamps

Work lamps suit a pared-down architectural interior, but also combine surprisingly well with more traditional styles of home. Old office and factory lamps from the 1940s and '50s, in iron or steel, often have beautiful shapes and a worn, industrial look. A single spotlight, fixed to the wall or clipped onto a shelf, makes a perfect reading light or can highlight a favorite picture.

Angled desk lamps are adjustable, stylish and functional. Their timeless and versatile design makes them ideal for table, bedside, and floor lighting. Standard versions are affordable; classic designs can be expensive, but are made of high-quality materials and are beautiful, so often well worth the investment.

Photography and film industry lighting equipment has been adapted for the domestic market. The simplest feature aluminum shades and clip-on fittings, and these are sometimes called loft lights. As they are movable, they can be attached to shelves and headboards, or to metal stands to transform them into floor lamps. These lamps are available in sophisticated designs and in high-quality materials; look for glass and color finishes.

Table and floor

Table and floor lamps give a subtle light which create a more subdued and cozy ambience. Shapes and styles vary from the traditional lamp base with a paper shade to minimalist metal stems topped with glass shades. Paper lamps provide a soft glow, while curvaceous, retro-style lamps add character. Don't be afraid to use a decorative or colorful lamp; it will add a personal touch and temper any cold or stark effects.

Kitchens

The kitchen has evolved from being merely a place for preparing and cooking food to being the center of social activity. Like any other room in the home, it exhibits the personality of its inhabitants. Some kitchens are disciplined and minimal; others show evidence of family life or a love of cooking and entertaining. A continuity of materials and color will maintain a clean-looking background for an area that has to accommodate and serve a number of needs, from food preparation and storage to washing dishes.

The choice of kitchen styles is diverse and ever expanding. Personal taste, lifestyle, the shape and size of the space, compatibility with the character of the property, and available budget are among the many factors to be considered. The influence of restaurant style is apparent in many contemporary domestic kitchens. Catering-style kitchens, with their industrial-size ranges, large expanses of countertop, and large sinks, look efficient and businesslike. Wood and natural stone look warm, yet practical, while concrete and stainless steel are cool and streamlined. To keep the look simple, choose restrained designs and plain cabinets and shelves—don't be tempted by such add-ons as decorative plate rails or carved detailings and moldings. Use a material that will last and mature with age, rather than show wear or chip. If possible, spend a little extra to achieve timelessness and quality. That said, inexpensive can be chic. Replacing handles and work surfaces with more high-grade materials makes cheap kitchen units look smarter, and a medley of styles can be united under a single countertop.

fitted

unfitted

catering

worktables

surfaces

kitchens

Fitted

Most American kitchens—certainly all of those in new homes—are of this type, in which appliances are neatly incorporated into a uniform system of cabinets and countertops. The obvious benefit is that the kitchen is tailored to suit the space and your requirements, and the uniformity creates a simple, cohesive background. A wide choice of base units, drawers, cabinets, fixtures, shelves, and appliances can be put together in an almost unlimited variety of ways.

Help with planning is usually available from the retailer, but make sure you have some idea of how the kitchen will look in elevation—combinations that work well on a plan may not work in reality. When planning wall cabinets and fixtures, remember to keep them in line with the base units to ensure they look balanced. Cost depends on quality, choice of materials, and style, but employing a professional to build the kitchen is worth the financial outlay.

Unfitted

The "unfitted" or "European-style" kitchen has a more heterogeneous character. Each element is freestanding, and a piece of furniture rather than a "unit." The pieces are usually wider and longer than standard units. They include full-height storage and island work stations.

Not having to fix them to the wall is an advantage, especially if your walls are unsuitable or uneven. They are best positioned so that there is space around each piece.

Mixing styles is possible with unfitted units. A collection of storage items can work well together, even if they are of different materials and styles. Ideally, the pieces should be good quality, functional, or very beautiful. Antique, retro, and industrial designs can add character and charm. Consider unconventional pieces, too. School, hospital, and office furniture and equipment is often very suitable, generous in size, and generally well made.

oak and steel drawers

Consider the "alternative use" of pieces. For example, old pigeonholes or a row of lockers can serve as storage, and an old slate slab may become a worktop.

Catering styles

Now that restaurant kitchens are as stylish as restaurants, the professional catering style has spread to domestic interiors. The generous proportions, clean lines, shiny surfaces, and industrial detailing are very much in tune with modern design. Look at professional catering suppliers—many of them sell to the domestic market. Most catering units are freestanding and can be placed in a number of positions. Stainless-steel sink units and worktables can be found. The sizes are large, so you may need a big space to fully explore this approach.

Worktables

A worktable or island that combines sink, cooktop, storage, and countertop in one unit looks compact and streamlined. It can be placed in less-conventional areas, such as the center of the room. The most extravagant are sleek, stainless-steel versions on slender legs.

Surfaces

The available variety and quality of kitchen materials has increased enormously in recent years. Choice of work surface depends on a combination of aesthetic, practical, and cost factors. To keep a simple look, choose a material that matches or complements the floor or fixtures.

Materials such as wood, stone, slate, terrazzo, concrete, metal, and an ever-increasing range of composites and laminates are widely available. A number of flooring materials can also be used for countertops (see pages 20-1, 47, 182 and 201-2). Wood and stone surfaces will need initial treatments and regular maintenance to keep them in good condition, and many will develop an attractive patina with regular use. Laminates are easy to clean, and hard finishes, such as ceramic tiles, terrazzo, and polished granite, are highly

white and concrete fitted units

simple unfitted kitchen

practical. Stainless steel is popular, with zinc, concrete, and rubber being newer alternatives. Reclaimed wood, marble, and slate slabs add character and a warm "living" quality which works well with hard-edged modern faucets.

All work surfaces are prone to wear and can become stained and damaged through use. Take basic precautions by using chopping boards to protect against the inevitable scratches and stains, and trivets to avoid burns.

Some of the materials listed below can also be used for backsplashes. Tiles give a clean, professional look and will blend with most kitchen designs. Stainless-steel sheeting looks modern and stylish. Stone gives a softer, more expensive, and luxurious look. Using the same material for the countertop and the

backsplash will help to unify non-matching storage and appliances.

Laminates are readily available, relatively inexpensive, and easy to use. Composed of a hard layer of synthetic material which is laminated to a reconstituted wood base, they are easy to cut and fit, and are ideal for the preparation of food and general kitchen use. Available in different colors, finishes, and textures, including metallic, stone, and wood effects, they are an effective way to unite a group of unrelated units. If selected in the same color as the units and walls, laminates will blend easily into the background.

Wood gives a warm and mellow look to a kitchen. It enhances the style of old and traditional houses, can add character to new spaces,

and softens the hard lines and materials of metal appliances and modern units. Solid wood should be used, and a dense grain is efficient and hard-wearing.

Beech, maple, and oak will need to be treated, usually with boiled linseed oil, but teak has natural oils and requires less-frequent oiling. Sealing the wood helps to provide an easy-care, stain-resistant surface, but allowing this natural material to breathe and look after itself will enable it to develop an attractive, mature appearance (see also page 137).

Stone is another natural material that can look good in almost any style of interior. Slate and granite, with their dark coloring and hard surfaces, are ideal for countertops, but limestone is now frequently used to give a lighter, softer look

kitchens

(see also page 139). After an initial treatment to reduce the porosity, limestone will stay clean with regular wiping down and, as with floors, will develop an attractive patina and eventually look after itself. Care must be taken to avoid contact with lemon juice, which "burns" into the surface, leaving stains that defy removal.

Concrete countertops are usually cast on site. To be robust and hygienic, the mixture needs to be specially formulated, and the surface will usually be polished to decrease the porosity.

Stainless steel has clean edges and a cool simplicity that will give a sharp, modern feel to a kitchen. It is a good functional material which is easy to clean, hygienic, and highly light-reflective. A sink and countertop can be formed from a single sheet—with no seams or sharp edges, it looks smart and architectural.

Stainless steel does mark and can become slightly duller and scratched with use. Regular maintenance involving special polishes will maintain its new finish, but the more muted sheen that develops in time is also attractive. If you are a keen cook and like a kitchen to look well-used, you may appreciate this softer effect.

Zinc has a wonderful dull sheen which works well with wood and provides an unusual and more subtle alternative to shiny stainless steel. Manufactured in sheets, it is normally wrapped around the edges of a work surface. The surface will mark and stain if it is not treated, but the material forms

tiled backsplashes

marble countertop

a patina with use. A sealant is usually applied to prevent excess damage, but a completely impervious coating gives an artificial, unnatural look.

Rubber is sometimes used as a work surface and is, in fact, highly practical. Used mainly in sheet form, it is inset into a metal or wooden surround. Resistant to heat and spills, and easy to clean, its matte finish and soft surface are sympathetic to most styles of kitchen, from the traditional to the very modern.

Composites, such as terrazzo, are formed from mixes of ground or powdered materials combined with pigments and bonding agents. The method of production produces a more consistent finish than natural materials, and the material has its own quality and character.

Available as tiles or slabs, composites can also be molded

into one-piece sink and countertop units. Many companies offer flooring in the same material and finish. Molded composites have a smooth, matte finish and rounded edges. Chipping and cracking can be a problem, so commission an expert for advice and installation.

Tiles give an efficient and hard-edged look. Although not as suitable for counters, they provide a waterproof, easy-to-clean surface for backsplash areas. Tiles are available in both glazed and matte finishes (see also page 139).

Sinks

Sinks can be made in the conventional materials of porcelain and composites or plastic, but sourcing an old stone sink or custom-making a concrete surface will make your kitchen more unique. Composites and plastics are easy-care, but porcelain, stone, and concrete will chip if heavy items are accidentally dropped or banged against them. They are unforgiving to dropped china and glass, which will almost certainly break on contact.

Rectangular porcelain sinks, based on the traditional British "butler's sink," have straight lines, a pure white color, and boxy good looks that make them perfect for a simple style. Some are fitted into a wooden surround with a draining board, but in these cases the sink loses its clean, stark shape. Standing them on large, sturdy metal brackets enhances their shape, and placing them on a wood or zinc plinth looks new and unusual. Other shapes that incorporate a drainage surface are available, as are luxurious versions made with a matte finish.

Stone sinks are beautiful but can be impractical, as items easily break on the surface. Antique, characterful sinks can be found in architectural suppliers and salvage yards, and they have a wonderful patina of age. New stone sinks, often a single large bowl, will impart a rustic look.

Concrete sinks, usually made on site, look good on their own or as part of a work surface. They seem modern when used with polished concrete floors and hard-edged materials and fixtures, but also have a rugged appearance that is suited to less formal surroundings.

Stainless steel sinks are practical, good-looking, and come in a various permutations, from single round bowls to double sinks with integrated chopping boards. They

look neat and simple when set into the counter. New versions are smoothly molded into seamless top units, incorporating a draining area, work surface, and even backsplashes. Freestanding stainless-steel catering sinks can be surprisingly well priced.

Plastic and composite sinks are popular as they are available in a range of colors and finishes. However, some are a little cheap-looking and over-detailed. Solid sinks molded from composites can look stunning, especially when supported on a slender stainless-steel frame.

Faucets

A faucet that swivels to serve two sinks is the most popular style. The simplest designs look like laboratory taps—tall and slender, curving into a graceful arc. Some versions have a spray attachment, which is useful for rinsing vegetables and washing dishes.

The choice between traditional knobs and levers depends on personal preference, though levers look smarter and will be easier for older, less nimble hands. Most faucets are made from chrome-plated metal or stainless steel, with a choice of shiny or satin finish, but colored lacquered metal is an alternative choice. High-tech modern faucets do not need to be limited to minimal kitchens; they will contrast wonderfully with old styles and materials.

Appliances

Ranges, refrigerators, freezers, washing machines, dishwashers, and microwaves are no longer necessarily white. Stainless steel

stainless steel open unit

mix of styles

has become a popular choice, as have combined units built into the wall and island units. To keep a streamlined look, choose all the appliances in the same solid color or finish, hide them behind cabinet doors, or relocate them to a pantry or utility room. Alternatively, in the case of a refrigerator or stove, make a bold statement with a freestanding retro style.

Built-in appliances, such as ovens, cooktops, and microwaves allow greater flexibility in the use of space. Available in stainless steel and white or colored enamel, they blend into a kitchen scheme and maintain a unified look.

Large industrial-style stoves and ranges can be found in most kitchen appliance stores. Their chunky shape suits the simple interior. New versions of old-fashioned enameled ranges have become popular. However, they

can look fussy, with too many knobs in shiny brass and exaggerated decorative features, so look for the plainer versions.

Specialist companies sell re-conditioned stoves and ranges. There are strict rules regarding the sale of secondhand appliances, so make sure the seller has the correct paperwork to verify its suitability. If you acquire a stove from another source, have it tested and approved as fit for use.

Solid range stoves—such as the Aga, a recent European import—have timeless good looks. They also heat water and can be used to run radiators. Some are very heavy, so you need to make sure the stove can be installed in your home. Choose white or black from among the many colors. These ranges usually become the heart of a home, a center of warmth and comfort, as well as a functional piece of equipment.

Bathrooms

For a simple style of bathroom, keep the surfaces practical and add touches of luxury or character. Function and efficiency are as important as appearance. The look should be pared-down without being cold or sterile. Many modern bathrooms have a "bathhouse" feel, with tiled floors and walls that are suited to contact with water and steam. As with kitchens, the variety of materials and hardware has increased enormously in the last few years. Luxury finishes, such as marble and granite, are now widely used for flooring, walls, bathtubs, and basins. For the inevitable splashing, choose surfaces and finishes that will not be damaged by contact with water.

Old-fashioned rectangular sinks (also known as "butler's sinks"), sometimes used in kitchens, can also be used in bathrooms where they fit in with traditional as well as contemporary settings. Modern designs for bath and sanitary ware are streamlined, and many are designed for small spaces. Small bathrooms can seem larger if they are efficient and plain, and their size may allow you to afford more expensive fixtures. Antique bathtubs and basins are available and can be reconditioned, but manufacturers also produce new versions based on old designs. Mixing styles is also possible—an old-fashioned bathtub can be placed alongside sleek, modern fixtures or a stone bowl placed next to a state-of-the art shower. A bathroom is also a good place to indulge in the unexpected or to make a feature of a decorative surface, such as exuberant wallpaper or a marble floor. Consider your lifestyle when planning a bathroom; an extra basin to cope with rush hours and family demands, or a separate shower in addition to a bathtub may be suitable options. Showers take up less space, but if you eliminate a bathtub entirely, you may miss the opportunity for relaxed candlelit bathing.

Basins

Basins and other sanitary ware are available in porcelain, natural stones, and composite materials. Glass basins and surrounds are best when plain, with bowls in clear or etched glass.

Some modern porcelain designs are elegant and streamlined, and there are ranges designed specifically for use in small spaces. For a simple style, choose a white color. An attractive industrial look can be achieved by placing a "butler's sink" on heavy-duty metal brackets or supporting it on a wood, stone, or distressed zinc plinth.

Limestone, marble, and slate are frequently used for bathroom surfaces and basins. A slab of limestone, custom-cut in a narrow wedge, can become a stunning, minimal basin. Stone basins look elemental, and marble surrounds are practical as well as chic. Basins molded from stone composites are seductively smooth and can be obtained in several subtle colors.

Old and antique basins have their own elemental appeal. Look for well-worn marble basins and large porcelain basins or sinks with high backsplashes or exaggerated detailing. New basins can be given an old-fashioned look by being set into a wooden surround or supported on a metal or wooden frame, as seen right.

Bathtubs

The old-fashioned bathtub on decorative feet is a timeless favorite. Look in salvage yards or specialist shops for genuine antiques. Many will have been re-enameled, and the outsides may have been resprayed a color. Stripping them down to the gray metal also looks good, but they will need to be sealed immediately with a clear lacquer to prevent rusting. The tubs can also be bought unrestored and then re-enameled and resprayed, and the dealer may offer this service. If you have inherited an antique tub, the enameling can be done in situ.

Manufacturers now reproduce some of the old shapes. Although these reproductions lack the character of the genuine article,

basin on wooden frame

bathrooms

they have a new, enameled surface and are made in a variety of standard sizes and colors. For a more modern look, consider alternatives to the traditional feet, such as resting the tub on slabs of rough-hewn wood or stone.

Showers

Bathrooms in modern houses and apartments include showers, either separately or combined with a tub, but if you have an old house, you may need to install one.

Before you do, make sure that the bathroom floor and surrounding surfaces are leak- and waterproof. Prevent water from splashing or seeping into areas where it might cause damage or staining to walls, floors, and the ceiling below. If you are installing a shower in a bedroom, an enclosure with floor and sides in one piece will minimize the chance of leakage.

Shower cabinets with glass doors can work well, but they may look obtrusive and might have corners and edges that are difficult to keep clean. Floor-to-ceiling tiles are an ideal waterproof surface (see page 190). Locating a shower in a recess or specially built space will keep splashes confined, and it may even be possible to do without a shower curtain.

Make sure your shower curtain is generous in length and width. Double curtains, such as a fabric or toweling curtain used with a separate waterproof liner, can be laundered and changed frequently.

Faucets

Even the most basic ranges of faucets and showerheads include "historic" styles, along with modern-looking designs, and they

porcelain sink on zinc

freestanding painted bathtub

double shower curtain

all have a choice of levers. Beautifully designed, luxury versions will enhance any style of bathroom and can make cheaper fixtures look more expensive.

The choice of style will depend on personal taste and the design of the fixtures, but don't be afraid to mix the clean lines and convenience of modern faucets with traditional shapes or the less-than-perfect surfaces of old tubs and basins. Faucets that come straight out of the wall look stylish, especially when used above a minimal basin. However, because the pipework is concealed behind the wall or panel, the installation will be a little more complicated and these faucets may be unsuitable for some bathrooms.

If you do want to use old faucets, which have plenty of character, make sure they have been reconditioned and work well. An old faucet soon loses its charm if it leaks or is difficult to turn on

and off. Whatever the style you choose, invest in good quality, especially for showerheads.

Accessories

Storage and accessories, from toothbrush holders to large cabinets, are obvious necessities. Keep to simple essentials in the same style and material. Avoid getting carried away by providing a place for everything, as the result may look cluttered. Store items out of sight in a wall cabinet, or display selected items neatly on shelves. Consider the details: cakes of soap look good in a wood or stone bowl, while plain hooks or pegs are useful for hanging towels.

Storage of some form is necessary in a bathroom. Most modern bathrooms contain adequate built-in storage for towels, toiletries, medicines, and all the other paraphernalia necessary for hygiene and health.

However, in an older house or apartment, you may need to add more. Cabinets can be built in, or you can buy a freestanding cabinet—perhaps an inexpensive, even quirky, piece of secondhand furniture. Old medical cabinets and dental storage units add a functional element to a bathroom, and simple wooden, country-style cupboards can be repainted to work with the decor.

Radiators and heated towel rails are convenient for extra warmth and for drying towels, and may be included in the bathroom. If possible, take advantage of new designs, which include tall spirals and clear glass panels. They can look stunning and dramatic in a bathroom, whereas they may not fit in elsewhere in the home. Towel rails can be fixed above ordinary radiators to help towels dry out, and heated towel rails can be obtained from specialist sources.

Storage

Storage plays an important role in the pursuit of clutter-free living. Even the most ardent non-materialist will have a surprising number of possessions for which to find a place. Think big; and don't be tempted by complicated storage systems and "solutions." Stowing items in one place or in one large piece of furniture is better than stashing smaller amounts in several locations or individual boxes, drawers, and sundry containers. An entire room devoted to storage, such as a dressing room or pantry, can help keep other rooms more spacious and streamlined. A large, free-standing armoire will hold a variety of objects; not only will they be easily accessible, but the armoire itself can be an attractive feature of the interior.

Built-in storage is discreet, as well as efficient, particularly if the design is plain and there are no handles or knobs. A contrasting finish, such as dark wood, will add visual interest while still maintaining a united front. Built-in kitchen and bathroom units can be designed to incorporate ample storage for all the relevant equipment, but adding extra cabinets—perhaps covering an entire wall—will provide space for less frequently used items.

walk-in

built-in

freestanding

containers

display

storage

Walk-in

Most modern homes have generous storage space, including one or more walk-in closets. These can often be made even more useful with the addition of extra shelves, shoe racks, or drawer units—ranging from ready-made items available at home centers to custom-made furniture, installed by a carpenter.

In older houses, closets may be small and inadequate. If you have, instead, plenty of rooms, consider converting a small bedroom into a dressing room and fitting it with storage units. Or, if a bedroom is exceptionally large, part of the area could be converted to this purpose, leaving a smaller but clutter-free area for sleeping and relaxing.

Built-in storage

An alternative, if you need more closet space, is to build a closet into the bedroom. Here again, options range from ready-made systems to custom carpentry. This solution can even improve the appearance of a room—by smoothing out awkward or oddly shaped spaces, for example. Custom-made built-in storage can

freestanding cupboard

metal lockers

be used in the living room, den, or office to house computers or entertainment centers.

A number of expensive, but extremely attractive, high-quality systems are now available in metal, etched glass, and beautiful wood finishes. If you choose a less expensive, self-assembly system, take care to install it properly; choose a simple design and substitute better-quality knobs and handles for those supplied.

Wall-size storage is a convenient way of maintaining order, and units can be constructed to become virtually invisible, especially if magnetic catches are used instead of knobs or handles. What appears to be a wood-paneled wall can actually be doors to closets or cabinets, as in the bathroom opposite, which houses clothes, towels, and linens behind wall-to-wall cabinets. Built-in storage that is confined to one wall may take up a lot of space, but the overall effect will make the room look pared down and simple .

A wall of cabinets, built as a "floating" or floor-to-ceiling partition, can be used to divide space and will keep all other walls clear. Concealing unsightly appliances behind a wall of doors will create order in a busy kitchen.

Freestanding units

Flexibility is the great advantage of freestanding storage items, such as chests of drawers and armoires, because you can arrange them within a space and take them with you when you move to a new home. They are ideal for storing large quantities of less-attractive necessities, including cooking utensils and food in a kitchen, files and a computer in an office, or tools and equipment in a workroom. They will keep dust away from china, glassware, and linens.

Used for concealing toys and paperwork, cabinets will enable a space to be reclaimed or re-invented after the children have gone to bed or office work is finished for the day. Many new cabinets are designed specifically for the storage of modern-day accoutrements, such as video and music systems.

The scale and style of large cabinets can be incorporated into most interiors. Antique armoires and linen presses have character and charm, as well as plenty of space. A single beautiful or unusual cabinet can become the focal point of an interior. Country-style cupboards sometimes look good with original, worn paintwork, but can also be repainted.

Utility cabinets, such as old school, office, factory, and hospital units, are usually large, well-made, and reasonably priced, and they can be cleaned or stripped and repainted or polished. Medical cabinets are often metal with glass doors, which makes them particularly suitable for bathrooms. Hospital suppliers sell new ones, but old painted metal versions have lots of character and are robust. If the paintwork is unacceptably "distressed," strip down to the bare metal and treat for rust or repaint.

Metal or wood lockers offer an unusual alternative. Find old ones from schools or institutions, or invest in new versions, which are available in a wide range of colors. Many companies that supply schools and leisure centers are happy to sell to individuals.

Chests of drawers may seem an obvious form of storage, but their attractiveness and efficiency are often overlooked in favor of more contemporary storage "solutions." Old and new versions are available in a variety of shapes, sizes, and prices, and they can be used for items as diverse as papers and files, craft materials, and clothing.

Containers

Lidded chests, trunks, boxes, and baskets are excellent for long-term storage, such as blankets, bed linens, and off-season clothes. Besides being visually pleasing, simply styled chests or trunks can supply additional opportunities for displaying objects or providing seating. Open baskets and boxes, perfect for toys and miscellaneous clutter, will work even better if fitted

wall of concealed cabinets

with casters so that they can be rolled away out of sight.

Containers in basketwork, plastic, or wood can provide tidy uniformed storage for regularly used items. Identical containers can be arranged in a series on windowsills or shelves, or hung on hooks. A row of wooden, wicker, or canvas boxes will provide under-bed storage and maintain a unified look.

Display

Remember that not everything needs to be hidden away. While many items will benefit from being kept out of sight—for practical as well as aesthetic reasons—storage often involves display as well as concealment. A home without evidence of personal tastes and pleasures will look cold and sterile. Also, you will be less inclined to use items if they are stored away. Keep an edited selection of magazines, home decorations, and often-used items on view.

Glass-fronted cabinets, consoles, and bookcases will show off your most valued possessions or collections and keep them orderly and dust free.

Shelving

Shelving is a popular and effective method of combining storage and display. For a minimal style, use "floating shelves," which have no visible means of support to interfere with their clean lines. Built-in shelving looks neat, especially in alcoves where the shelves are cut to fit the space. Adjustable shelving systems are flexible and easy to install, and the brackets and other hardware are often covered by the contents, although brackets and supports are part of the design in many modern high-tech systems. Using different materials with decorative or unusual brackets can turn a shelf into a feature, and serendipitous finds, such as ornate wall units and old-fashioned plate racks, can add charm and light relief to an otherwise disciplined environment.

Single shelves can be built at high or low level to continue the established lines of the interior. For a cohesive arrangement, display either a small number of carefully chosen objects or small groups of items in similar colors or styles where you can see and appreciate them. Open shelving allows immediate access and will look organized if items are sorted by category and a full wall is devoted to the shelves. Freestanding units and bookcases can cover unsightly or irregular walls and work well in certain styles, scales, or structures of interior. A wall of books has a "library" feel, which is visually pleasing and looks much simpler than assorted bookcases.

shelving

Floating shelves

Without supports or brackets to detract from their simplicity, floating shelves are elegant and modern. They can be used singly or in rows and can be purchased in a limited range of sizes from large furniture stores or home centers, ready to install, or can be custom-built by a carpenter.

Floating shelves are usually made from a single thick piece of solid wood with drilled holes which slots onto bolts or dowels fixed into the wall. Alternatively, the shelves are formed from several sections of wood—usually veneered, lacquered, or ready-to-paint plywood—to form a thicker construction which fits over a batten screwed to the wall.

Despite their lightweight construction, floating shelves can support a lot of weight, depending on the hardware used and the structure of the wall. Long screws are usually needed to support shelves for heavy items, such as books, and partition walls need special anchor-type metal fasteners which open up behind the panel to grip it.

Built-in shelves

Normally fitted into alcoves, built-in shelving makes maximum use of the space. When painted or finished to match the walls, shelves will blend into the structure of the room, rather than standing out as an addition. Installation will require careful measuring, but a professional carpenter can fit shelves to your specifications.

Materials for shelving should be chosen for the function of the shelves and the structure of the walls. To prevent shelves on wide spans from sagging under heavy loads, a thicker material is needed.

Solid wood looks best, even when painted. Softwoods, such as pine, are relatively inexpensive and therefore widely used, but for a more distinctive look, use large slabs of hardwood, such as oak or beech. Consider using a dark stain on thick softwood shelves to emulate the effect of hardwood.

Various types of plywood can be used for shelving. "Interior" plywoods, which are faced with hardboard, are especially suitable for this purpose.

floating shelves

Fixtures will depend on the width of the span. For short spans, shelves can be fixed onto battens attached to the side walls, but for long spans, battens on all three sides may be required. Battens need to be cut shorter than the depth of the shelf, and the corners must be cut away to keep them concealed. Alternatively, a narrow strip can be fixed across the front to hide the batten, as well as to add thickness to the shelf.

If the shelves are placed high up or far apart, the battens may still be visible. Painting them to blend with the wall will minimize their impact. Slim, metal brackets, which fix to the side walls so that only a narrow right angle of metal is seen, are also available.

Shelving systems

Modern, elegant shelving systems can be found in a range of materials and prices. Some have glass shelves and slender metal supports that look clean and minimal, whereas others appear industrial and high-tech. They look effective when covering a wall or in a narrow floor-to-ceiling column.

Utility metal shelving systems, used in retailers and warehouses and sold by catering suppliers, are now widely available for domestic use. The most common form have mesh shelves that fit together with tubular uprights. They can be bought in sections, with a choice of shelf widths and depths, and adapted to fit any space. Their functional look, large scale, and shiny finish make an impact. Other catering units in stainless steel can also be sourced.

Galvanized shelving systems, available from industrial suppliers, have adjustable shelves with angled steel uprights and can be ordered in any length or size.

Luxury, upscale shelving systems are sophisticated and expensive, but highly versatile. They can be attached to the wall or supported on uprights between the floor and

long, low shelving

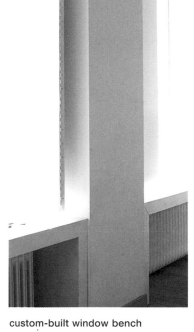

custom-built window bench

picture shelf

ceiling. They work well as room dividers, and the variety of components, including desk shelves and cabinets, enables them to be used in work spaces or kitchens.

Inexpensive self-assembly systems can also be used successfully. Some have metal brackets that slot into metal strips fixed to the wall. They are easy to install and effective in a recess, where the shelves can be cut to the same width and depth to give a built-in look. Many have the advantage of being adjustable, in order to accommodate different or changing groups of objects. Though superseded by more sophisticated systems, they do have an honest simplicity that can work well in a pared-down interior.

Single shelves

A single shelf can be both functional and decorative—a

simple way of providing extra storage or an opportunity to display a collection of objects. For storage purposes, a long, single shelf will be more effective than tiers of shorter ones. In a kitchen, a long shelf is useful for providing easy access to frequently used china, glassware, pots, and pans. Long, low, wide shelving can provide seating or display, with areas underneath for storage. Alternatively, a shelf can run the length of a wall to provide additional work space in a kitchen or office.

On an otherwise bare wall, a single shelf can become a focal point, and a floating version will look particularly modern and understated. In a simple setting, a decorative shelf unit—perhaps an antique market find—can look charming and unexpected. A slab of slate or other unusual material supported on ornate brackets also adds character.

Install a picture shelf to provide a place for displaying photographs, plates, or other objects. A narrow wood or metal shelf is ideal for an eye-level collection, which can be changed frequently. A slender strip of aluminum can also be set into a plastered wall, as seen above. If you are using a narrow shelf, make sure it is wide enough to prop objects at a safe angle and that the shelf has a small lip to keep the items in place.

Freestanding units

Inexpensive freestanding shelves and bookcases are available in a range of styles and materials. Choose white or pale wood finishes, or repaint the shelves, if necessary. Wooden shelving systems, with the uprights and shelves bought separately, do not have to be attached to the wall. Although rather basic in design, they will be less noticeable if painted to blend in with the walls.

Furnishings

There are no rules when it comes to simple style furnishings. The emphasis is on using furniture carefully and sparingly, disposing of unnecessary items or disguising unattractive ones, or replacing them with more streamlined versions. All styles of furniture can be incorporated, from the pared-down lines of contemporary design to the charming and characterful look of old pieces. It is not compulsory to keep to one style; the modern approach is an eclectic one, in which combinations of old and modern, traditional and ethnic, plain and decorative, cheap and expensive, can work together. The traditional boundaries between cooking, eating, relaxing, and working have now virtually disappeared, and furnishings may need to be multifunctional. Tables work well as desks, sofas may be turned into beds, and large cabinets can house computers. Your lifestyle and personal taste will, of course, influence your choice of furnishings, but comfort should not be sacrificed for style.

blending

choosing

renovation

furnishings

Blending styles

The key to creating a simple look is to blend furnishings by choosing sympathetic materials, colors, shapes, and textures. A sleek modern sofa, a battered old box, and an ethnic stool will happily coexist in the same room. Hard-edged modern can rub shoulders with faux fur, and antiques can harmonize with chain-store chairs and designer lamps. The exuberant shapes and colors of retro styles often mix well with chain-store bargains, and the decorative excesses of period pieces will be tempered if they are placed in isolation within a calm, monochrome environment.

Contrasting styles work well and sit comfortably together when the surroundings are understated or when pieces are linked by similar colors, shapes, or fabrics. For example, a disparate group of chairs can be unified by painting all the chairs white, but the chairs will also work together if they are made of the same wood or covered in similar types of fabric.

Design classics by Le Corbusier, Marcel Breuer, Charles and Ray Eames, and Arne Jacobsen, among many others, are now fully appreciated for their clean lines,

beautiful curves, and imaginative use of materials. Many of these designs are still being produced, but the originals are much sought after and may be sourced in outlets specializing in retro pieces. Other quirky pieces from the past, often at relatively low prices, can also be found at these retailers.

Contemporary designs in good-quality materials have recently become more widely available. The expanding interest in modern furniture has resulted in stores selling bigger ranges by new and established designers. However, the availability of good modern design is no longer confined to upscale interiors stores; most large furniture companies stock contemporary ranges at mid-price, while some retailers specialize in selling well-designed furniture and home accessories at low cost.

Antique and secondhand furniture can be found in good condition at house sales, antique markets, and fairs, both nationally and abroad. Beautiful antiques or old furniture with a timeless quality will fit in with any style. Simple utilitarian pieces have character and are generally inexpensive. Stores and salvage yards specializing in house

antique iron bedstead

clearance often have good-quality plain furniture that cannot be readily identified as belonging to any special era, but will have an honest charm of its own, and may simply require a coat of paint. If you have spotted a trend that hasn't yet reached the specialist stores, you may be able to get in early with some great bargains. Look for country-style pieces, such as metal bed frames, simple tables, and small cabinets.

Ethnic furniture can work well with a simple interior, where it can be fully appreciated against a plain background or as part of a small collection. The increase in foreign travel has exposed us to a wide spectrum of styles and products from other cultures. Traveling abroad is not necessary, though; many local stores sell ethnic pieces from such places as Europe, Africa, India, and the Far East. Specialist dealers are a good source for more unusual or sophisticated examples.

Choosing furnishings

Keeping it simple means fewer pieces of furniture; ideally, everything should earn its place by being beautiful, comfortable, and functional. Although it is not always possible for all these criteria to be met—for cost, practical, or sentimental reasons—they can help when choosing new furnishings or deciding which ones to eliminate. Any beautiful piece will usually fit in; but if it is distinctive or decorative, you may need to restrain other elements in order to allow it to stand out.

Useful furniture to own includes storage cabinets, bookcases, cabinets with glass doors for display, sofas that double up as beds, tables that can be used as desks, and chests that can also serve as seats or coffee tables.

Scale is an important consideration with furniture, not only for the practical reason of whether a piece will fit the available space, but also for aesthetic reasons: does it work with the proportions of the room and the rest of the contents? A simple interior will highlight any discrepancies; but a piece of furniture that may have been considered too big or dominant in a cluttered environment can look perfect in a pared-down setting.

Basic materials used in the construction of furniture have widened in scope. More adventurous and unusual materials, such as plastics, glass, galvanized metal, and stainless steel, are now available, in addition to traditional wood and leather.

To create a simple style of interior, you will need to limit the number of elements used; but don't be too disciplined or else your scheme will lack personality. Polished wood, dull metal, and the weathered and worn surfaces of old leather and paintwork are mellow and characterful; pale woods, shiny metal, or aluminum, and the lacquered or plastic finishes of new furniture, look cool and sharp.

Upholstery in modern styles is chic and minimal and often makes a bold statement. When buying upholstered furniture, choose neutral colors—they look sophisticated, will blend readily with other pieces of furniture, and can easily be incorporated into new decorating schemes when you want a change. Alternatively, a bold sofa, daybed, or *chaise longue* can become a centerpiece and provide the basis for the interior design and color scheme of the room.

neutral modern daybed

No matter how wonderful chairs and sofas may look, they should be comfortable, too. When buying upholstered sofas or chairs, try them out in the store to make sure you can sit or lie in a relaxed position. If you have a piece that is blissfully comfortable, but not attractive, cover it in a neutral fabric and add beautiful cushions and throws to further disguise it, if necessary (see page 121).

Colors should be used in a controlled way for a simple style approach. To harmonize your furnishings with their surroundings, keep to a basic palette. Groups of naturals and neutrals, from pale grays to strong browns, always work well together and will benefit from the addition of textures. Alternatively, use a base of neutrals, but add one or two strong colors as accents. White may seem a good choice for a minimal look, but it stains easily.

Renovation

Old furniture, including antiques, junk-shop finds, and pieces you may have had for years, will benefit from regular cleaning, repairing, and restoring. Simple care and maintenance can give furniture a new lease on life. For serious renovation, there are specialist books and products on the market, but if you have valuable pieces, seek expert advice.

When renovating old furniture, be careful not to destroy its "character" through over-enthusiastic cleaning. Evidence of age and use is often attractive.

Natural wood will respond well to cleaning, oiling, and polishing. Use a mild detergent and water to remove dirt and old wax, and reveal the grain and original color. Though the result may look pale and dry, feeding the wood with fresh oil and wax, or even a little stain, will enhance it.

renovation
slipcovers
accessories
pictures

furnishings

painted new table

old leather armchair

Metal frames or legs on retro-style furniture can also be scrubbed clean, but don't rub too hard on painted metal or you will damage the finish. Scrubbing old metal that has been painted can often give an attractive "distressed" finish. To reveal the stark simplicity of bare metal, you will need to strip off all paint, using a commercial paint stripper if necessary, and rub down the surface with a wire brush or steel wool. A coat of sealant needs to be applied to the metal to prevent rust from forming.

Paintwork in good condition simply needs cleaning with a mild detergent and water, but painting or repainting a piece of furniture is a good way to give a fresh, new look, add character or blend a piece into the background.

Sometimes a piece of inexpensive furniture is well designed and attractive, but the color or quality of the material is incompatible with your interior. If this is the case, consider painting it in plain eggshell or gloss; a liberal application of white gloss paint can transform a plain wood table into a stylish object.

For a pristine finish on raw wood, first use a primer to provide an even base and prevent paint from soaking in. A fashionably "distressed" look can be created by painting directly onto the wood with a thin layer of latex paint. When dry, sand down the surface to reveal some of the wood beneath. Build up several thin layers, sanding down between each one, and seal with a coat of wax or varnish.

For a smooth finish on metal, first sand it down well to give an even surface, then paint it with a primer and enamel paints specified for use on metal.

Old leather has a wonderful mellow quality, and an old leather chair, even a very battered one, adds warmth and character to a room. Leather needs special care. Central heating will dry it out, and old leather will need to be revived and "fed" to keep it supple and prevent cracking. There are various treatments available for feeding leather, but avoid any oily product on chairs as it may subsequently damage clothes. Saddle soap is a traditional treatment, and very dry leather may require several initial applications and regular treatments thereafter.

Upholstery can be cleaned using one of the many suitable upholstery cleaners on the market, but there are also professional companies who will do the job quickly and thoroughly. If the upholstery is very worn, it will need to be replaced. Although you can do this yourself, using the services of a professional upholsterer gives the best result.

Slipcovers

New slipcovers will transform even the dullest of furniture. As fabrics play an important role in creating the right look, the effect can be quite dramatic. Fitted or tailored covers involve accurate measuring, sewing, and securing. Loose slipcovers, however, are easier to make and suit a more relaxed feel.

Choose solid colors—perhaps with a woven texture—or simple patterns, such as checks or stripes. Neutral covers can be used to smarten up an old sofa or lessen the impact of a large or unattractive one. Choosing a selection of fabrics in a similar type, color, or tone for a group of chairs and sofas will unify them without looking too considered. Unexpected contrasts work well, such as using monogrammed antique linens to cover a retro piece or soften the shape of a modern one. Covering a traditional sofa in an unexpected material, such as denim or ticking, will give it an up-to-date identity.

Casual-fit slipcovers are easy to make, as they do not have to be a perfect fit. They work well on fully upholstered armchairs and sofas. Simplest of all is a large throw, but unless it is of a substantial material, it can look untidy as soon as anyone sits down.

Tie-on covers are perfect for dining chairs and armchairs without solid arms, but can be used on any style of furniture. Furniture shape will influence the style of the cover, but tie-ons can usually be made with straight seams and flaps rather than complicated constructions.

fitted slipcovers

tie-on covers

simple cushions

Accessories

Finishing touches bring color, texture, and a touch of luxury and extravagance to restrained interiors. A mix of textures can be built up using layers of fabrics in complementary tones, and mixing solids with prints or antique linens with lace can look charming.

Cushions knitted in soft wools, such as cashmere, and in both bulky and fine yarns, are warm and tactile. Faux fur, suede, and velvet add luxury and comfort to a hard-edged interior. Felted wool, flannel, and woven tweeds look tailored and smart. White cotton or linen gives a fresh appearance. Use cushions sparingly—a large cushion looks much more chic than a scattering of smaller ones.

Throws, blankets, and quilts introduce softness and warmth to a minimal interior and add a decorative element. They can be draped over armchairs, sofas, or beds. Look for faux fur and quilted throws, and those with a contrasting lining or edging. Velvet, cashmere, and wool throws drape well and can also be used as comforting wraps in chilly weather. Cream wool blankets with blanket-stitched edges and stripes or windowpane checks look suitably simple. Antique quilts, whether newly purchased or treasured heirlooms, are usually beautifully sewn and have a timeless quality, and new quilts are sometimes made in velvets, silks, and satins.

Bed linens in white cotton or linen always look fresh and inviting, and pale beiges and grays are more sophisticated. In a pared-down bedroom, brightly colored linen is cheerful, especially on children's beds. Ginghams and floral prints work especially well when used only for pillowcases, a bed skirt, or a bottom sheet.

Antique linens have a special handmade quality that makes them soft and wonderful to sleep on. They wash and bleach well, and there are coarse or fine versions. Old linen sheets made into curtains will hang beautifully; made into loose slipcovers, they give a fresh but relaxed look.

Pictures

Pictures reflect your passions and preferences, and photographs provide evidence of your life and loves. They can be propped against the wall or floor, or on a mantelpiece or shelf. If you intend to display lots of pictures, keep the interior relatively disciplined. The frames or subject matter should be consistent. Simple frames blend, but an ornate or unusual one can serve as a focus. One or two large pictures can look dramatic if the colors are bold, but the effect can be subtle and restful when colors harmonize.

Accessories

CHATEAU EDGEWATER INC
PO Box 2436
Wilsonville, OR 97070
tel (503) 682 8569
fax (503) 570 2737
email: BDreisse@msn.com
www.chateauedgewater.com
Baskets, trunks

CRATE & BARREL
1860 West Jefferson Avenue
Naperville, Illinois 60540
tel (1 800) 967 6696
www.crateandbarrel.com
Furniture and accessories, retail and mail order

KEEPSAKE QUILTING
Route 25B
Center Harbor, NH 03226
tel (800) 525 8086
fax (603) 253 83 46
email: customerservice@
 keepsakequilting.com
www.keepsakequilting.com
'America's Largest Quilt Shop' - retail and online shopping

MK SWORKS LTD
PO Box 1057
Marlborough, MA 01752
tel (508) 624 6311
fax (508) 624 6309
email: info@mksworks.com
www.mksworks.com
Quilts, pillows, hangings in the New England style

NEIMAN MARCUS
150 Stockton Street
San Francisco, CA 94108
tel (415) 362 3900
tel (1 888) 888 47 57 for online
customer services
www.neimanmarcus.com
Department store and online shopping

RALPH LAUREN HOME COLLECTION
1185 Sixth Avenue
New York, NY 10036
tel (800) 377 7656
email: customersupport@polo.com
www.polo.com
rlhome.polo.com

SantaFe INTERIORS
214 Old Sante Fe Trail
Sante Fe, NM 87501
tel (800) 391 7928
fax (323) 935 1561
www.santefeinteriors.com
Hand woven rugs, bedspreads, textiles made in collaboration with the Zapotec Indians

TOAST
D Lakeside
Llansamlet
Swansea
SA7 9FF, UK
tel +44 (0) 870 240 5200
email: contact@toastbypost.co.uk
www.toastbypost.co.uk
Bedlinens, blankets and quilts, mail order and online

WA
184 Commercial Street
Provincetown, MA 02657
tel (508) 487 6355
tel (888) 799 6355
fax (508) 487 6844
email: wa@waharmony.com
www.waharmony.com
Oriental accessories

WOLFMAN GOLD & GOOD INC
117 Mercer Street
New York, NY 10012
tel (212) 1888

Antiques/Retro Furniture

www.antiqueshopsusa.com
email: info@antiqueguide.net
useful web directory

AMAZING EMPORIUM
249 Cricklewood Broadway
London
NW2 6NX, UK
tel +44 (0) 20 8208 1616
fax +44 (0) 20 8450 4511
email:sales@
 amazingemporium.com
www.amazingemporium.com
furniture and accessories online catalog

CIRCA 50
Manchester, VA
tel (1 877) 247 2250
www.circa50.com
Catalog available for ordering online or by phone

CHERNER CHAIR CO
PO Box 2689
Westport, CT 06880
tel (866) 243 7637
fax (203) 431 8994
email: mail@chernerchair.com
www.chernerchair.com

COGAN'S ANTIQUES
110 South Palmer Street
Ridgeway, SC 29130
tel (803) 337 3939
email: john@cogansantiques.com
www.cogansantiques.com

JEAN GESTAS, S.A.
Route Dept. 48
Came, 64520
France
tel (978) 369 5222
fax (978) 369 2992
email: info@gestas.com
www.gestas.com
*Reproductions of French country
furniture*

PHILLIPS AUCTIONEERS
3 West 57th Street
New York, NY 10019
tel (212) 940 1200
fax (212) 688 1647
www.phillips-auctions.com

PICKWICK ANTIQUES
3851 Interstate Court
Montgomery, AL 36109
tel (334) 279 1481
tel (1 800) 236 7138
fax (334) 279 1486
www.pickwckantiques.com

POOR RICHARD'S RESTORATIONS
Montclair, NJ
tel (973) 783 5333
fax (973) 744 1939
email: Jrickford@webtv.net
www.rickford.com

Architectural Salvage and Reclamation

ARCHITECTURAL SALVAGE
www.salvo.com
*Website for specialists in
architectural salvage and reclaimed
building materials*

ARCHITECTURAL SALVAGE INC
3 Mill Street
Exeter, NH 03833
tel (603) 773 5635
fax (603) 773 5635
email: arch@ttlc.net
www.oldhousesalvage.com

**THE ORIGINAL RECLAMATION
TRADING CO LTD**
22 Elliott Road
Love Lane Estates
Cirencester, Gloucestershire
GL7 1YS, UK
tel +44 (1) 285 653 532
fax +44 (1) 285 644 383
www.theoldhouseweb.com
*Comprehensive directory of
products and suppliers*

Bathrooms

EUROBATH & TILE
Stonemill Design Center
2915 Redhill Avenue
Suite F-102
Costa Mesa, CA 92626
tel (714) 545 22 84
fax (714) 957 2691
email: sales@eurobathandtile.com
www.eurobathtile.com
*Bath and kitchen fixtures - stone
and tile*

FIREWORKS TILES
9 Wilson Street
Amissville, VA 20106
tel (540) 937 8944
fax (540) 937 8949
email:customerservices@
  fireworkstiles.com
www.fireworkstiles.com
*Handpainted and handcrafted
kitchen and bathroom tiles*

SPRING HOUSE SPECIALITY CO
1303 Gravel Pike, Box 271
Zieglerville, PA 19492
tel (610) 287 8841
fax (610) 287 7082
www.springhousenet.com
*Manufacturers of decorative
plumbing items such as old
fashioned leg tubs, etc.*

WINSTAR
1252 Hibiscus Lane
Apopka, FL 32703
tel (407) 869 9469
fax (407) 869 1351
email: assistance@
  luxuryhomeproducts.com
www.winstar.org
*Bathroom and kitchen plumbing
products*

Fabrics

BRUNSCHWIG & FILS
available through your interior
designer
www.brunschwig.com
Furniture, fabric and accessories

CHASE ERWIN
c/o Zoffany
979 Third Avenue, Suite 1403
New York, NY 10022
tel (212) 593 9787
fax (212) 593 9771
www.chase-erwin.co.uk
Silk and silk fabrics

DESIGNERS GUILD
c/o Osborne & Little Inc
979 Third Avenue, Suite 250
New York, NY 10022
tel (212) 751 3333
fax (212) 752 6027
email: info@designersguild.com
www.designersguild.com

directory

floors
heating
kitchens
lighting and
furniture

F SCHUMACHER & CO
79 Madison Avenue
New York, NY 10016
tel (212) 415 3900
fax (212) 415 3907
www.fschumacher.com

LEE JOFA INC
201 Central Avenue South
Bethpage, NY 11714
tel (800) 453 3563
tel (516) 752 7600
fax (516) 752 9623
email:customer.service@
   leejofa.com
www.leejofa.com

OPPENHEIM'S
PO Box 29
120 East Main Street
North Manchester, IN 46962-0052
tel (800) 461 6728
Fabrics including denim

OSBORNE & LITTLE
979 Third Avenue
New York, NY 10022
tel (212) 751 3333
fax (212) 752 6027
www.osborneandlittle.com
For stockists nationwide

ZOFFANY
Suite 1403, D&D Building
979 Third Avenue
New York, NY 10022
tel (1 800) 395 8760
tel (770) 438 8760
fax (770) 432 6215
www.zoffany.com

Floors

Bedrosians
4285 N. Golden State Blvd
Fresno, CA 93722-6316
tel (559) 275 5000
fax (559) 275 1753
email: bedrosians@aol.com
www.bedrosians.com
*Showrooms in California, Nevada,
Arizona, Colorado and Florida
Ceramic tile and natural stone*

CRAFTSMAN LUMBER CO INC
435 Main Street
PO Box 222
Groton, MA 01450
tel (978) 448 5621
fax (978) 448 2754
email: mark@craftsmanlumber.com
www.craftsmanlumber.com
*Specialists in wide pine and oak
flooring, paneling and custom
millwork*

CRUCIAL TRADING
PO Box 11
Duke Place
Kidderminster
Worcestershire
DY10 2JR, UK
tel +44 (0) 1562 820 006
fax +44 (0) 1562 823 0030
www.crucial-trading.com
for US stockists
*Natural floor coverings, including
coir, sisal, seagrass, jute, wool and
marmoleum*

HOSKING HARDWOOD FLOORING
PO Box 163
Walpole, MA 02081
tel (508) 668 8315
tel (877) 356 6755 for orders
www.hoskinghardwood.com

JAMES E HARVEY MILLWORK INC
PO Box 249
22665 River Ridge Road
Bozman, MD 21612-0249
tel (410) 822 7689
fax (410) 745 9926
email: info@harveymillwork.com
www.harveymillwork.com
*Custom flooring, stair parts and
paneling*

JOHNSON
H&R Johnson Tiles Ltd
Highgate Tile Works
Tunstall
Stoke-on-Trent
ST6 4JX, UK
tel +44 (0) 1782 575 575
fax +44 (0) 1782 577 377
www.johnson-tiles.com
for US stockists
Ceramic tiles for floors and walls

PERGO, Inc
Attention: Consumer Affairs
3128 Highwoods Blvd.
Suite 100
Raleigh, NC 27604
tel (1 800) 337 3746
email: pergomail@casupport.com
www.pergo.com
useful website for laminate flooring

SIMPSON STONE TILE
423 W. Columbia Street
Orlando, FL 32825
tel (407) 481 1066
fax (407) 737 6008
*Reproductions with the natural
looks of slate, terra cotta, rustic,
marble, etc.*

Heating

ARSCO

3564 Blue Rock Road

Cincinnati, OH 452 47

tel (800) 543 7040

email: arsco@arscomfg.com

www.arscomfg.com

Radiator covers

BUCKLEY RUMFORD FIREPLACES

1035 Monroe Street

Port Townsend, WA 98368

tel (800) 447 7788

fax (360) 385 1624

email: buckley@rumford.com

www.rumford.com

THE CHIMNEY SWEEP INC

913 Harris Avenue

Bellingham, WA 98225

tel (888) 354 6733

tel (360) 676 8585

fax (360) 676 9080

email:mail@

   chimneysweeponline.com

www.chimneysweeponline.com

'Antique look' kitchen appliances,

gas and wood stoves

DIAMOND W PRODUCTS

30 Railroad Avenue

Albany, NY 12205

tel (518) 459 6775

fax (518) 459 3623

email: rfdw@msn.com

www.diamond-w.com

Ready-made and custom-made

fireplace door enclosures and hearth

heaters for wood and gas fires

THELIN COMPANY INC

PO Box 847

Nevada City, CA 95959

tel (800) 949 5048

tel (530) 273 1976

fax (530) 273 3707

email: sales@thelinco.com

www.thelinco.com

Gas and pellet stoves

TULIKIVI US INC

One Penn Plaza

Suite 3600

New York, NY 10119

tel (212) 896 3897

fax (212) 760 1088

www.tulikivi.com

unique stone fireplaces from

England

Kitchens

AGA RANGES LLC

110 Woodcrest Road

Cherry Hill, NJ 08003

tel (800) 633 9200

email: info@aga-ranges.com

www.aga-ranges.com

ALNO

A.N.U.

One Design Center Place

Suite 643

Boston, MA 02210

tel (617) 482 2566

email: gadit@alno.com

www.alno.com

German kitchen manufacturer with

worldwide distribution

BALTHAUP KITCHENS

www.balthaup.com

for US stockists and showrooms

CHALON

c/o Oliver Walker & Company

1855 Griffin Road, Suite A423

Dania, FL 33004

tel (954) 929 0031

www.chalon.com

for showrooms nationwide

GAGGENAU

tel (800) 294 0644

www.gaggenau.com

for stockists nationwide

Built-in appliances

IKEA

www.ikea.com

www.ikea-usa.com

for nearest outlet. Some products

available via home shopping

KNOBS BY NATURE

27916 NE Zinser Road

Battle Ground, WA 98604

tel (360) 666 0746

www.knobsbynature.com

Kitchen and bathroom knobs

handcrafted from river rocks

PLAIN AND SIMPLE KITCHENS

Kitchen Living LLC

One Design Center Place

Suite 620

Boston, MA 02210

tel (617) 439 8800

www.plainandsimplekitchens.com

RESTORATION HARDWARE

711 Boylston Street

Boston, MA 02116

tel (617) 578 0088

www.restorationhardware.com

Functional and decorative

hardware, plus home furnishings -

retail and online shopping

SIEMATIC

www.siematic.co.uk

for US stockists and showrooms

WATTS AND WRIGHT

Showrooms nationwide

tel +44 (8) 700 110 130

tel +44 (1) 922 622 249

fax +44 (1) 922 648 100

email:dealerships@

  wattsandwright.com

www.wattsandwright.com

Bespoke cabinetmakers

WILLIAMS-SONOMA

Stanford Shopping Center

180 El Camino Real

Palo Alto, CA 94304

tel (650) 321 3486

www.williams-sonoma.com

Kitchen equipment and home

furnishings retailer - also online/

mail order

WINSTAR

1252 Hibiscus Lane

Apopka, FL 32703

tel (1 888) 880 9469 for orders

tel (407) 869 9469

fax (407) 869 1351

email: assistance@

  luxuryhomeproducts.com

www.winstar.org

Lighting and Furniture

The Bon Marché

1601 3rd Avenue

Seattle, WA 98181

tel (206) 506 6000

www.thebonmarche.com

Department store

THE CRAFTSMAN HOMES

CONNECTION

PMB 343

2525 E. 29th Street

Suite 10B

Spokane, WA 99223

tel (509) 535 5098

fax (509) 534 8916

email: Elvis@crafthome.com

www.crafthome.com

THE CONRAN SHOP

Bridgemarket

407 East 59th Street

New York, NY 10022

tel (212) 755 9079

fax (212) 888 3008

www.conran.com

Modern furniture, lighting, fabrics

and accessories

ETHAN ALLEN

PO Box 1966

Danbury, CT 0681-1966

tel (203) 743 8000

fax (203) 243 8298

www.ethanallen.com

ISGRO & COMPANY

3248 Sacramento Avenue

San Francisco, CA 94115

tel (415) 931 5858

Antique lighting, restoration, repair

and design

LIGNE ROSET

250 Park Avenue

New York, NY 10003

tel (212) 375 1036

fax (212) 375 1039

email: info@ligne-roset-usa.com

info@lignerosetny.com

www.ligne-roset.com

www.lignerosetny.com

French furniture and design, outlets

nationwide

MACY'S WEST

170 O'Farrell Street

San Francisco, CA 94102

tel (415) 397 3333

www.macys.com

Department store

PIER 1 IMPORTS

For a store in your area call

(800) 447 4371

THE POTTERY BARN

Retail or mail order

tel (888) 779 5176

fax (702) 363 2541

www.potterybarn.com

THE RENOVATOR'S SUPPLY

Renovator's Old Mill

Millers Falls, MA 01349

tel (800) 659 2211

fax (413) 659 3796

www.renovatorssupply.com

mail order and online

WD BOSWORTH WOODWORKING &

SCULPTURE

59 Luther Warren Drive

St Helena Island, SC 29920

tel (843) 838 9490

fax (843) 838 1187

email: woodwork@hargray.com

www.qualitywoodworking.com

Custom furniture using traditional

joinery techniques and quality wood

REJUVENATION LAMP

& FIXTURE CO

2550 NW Nicolai Street

Portland, Or 97210

tel (888) 343 8548

fax (800) 526 7329

email: info@rejuvenation.com

www.rejuvenation.com

Period lighting

paints

planning

storage

windows

directory

Paints

ARTHUR SANDERSON & SONS LTD
Suite 409
979 Third Avenue
New York, NY 10022
tel (212) 319 7220
fax (212) 593 6184
www.sanderson-uk.com
Traditional English paints and
wallpapers, including William Morris
prints

BENJAMIN MOORE & CO
51 Chestnut Ridge Road
Montvale, NJ 07645
tel (1 800) 344 0400
email: info@benjaminmoore.com
www.benjaminmoore.com
to use their online colour selector

THE OLD FASHIONED MILK PAINT
CO INC
436 Main Street
Groton, MA 01450
tel (978) 448 6336
fax (978) 448 2754
email: sales@milkpaint.com
www.milkpaint.com
For building or restoring Colonial or
Shaker furniture

FARROW AND BALL
Uddens Estate
Wimborne
Dorset
BH21 7NL, UK
tel +44 (0) 1202 876 141
fax +44 (0) 1202 873 793
www.farrow-ball.com
for information on buying direct
from UK or list of US stockists
Traditional paints and wallpapers

PAINT AND PAPER LIBRARY
Fonthill Ltd
979 Third Avenue
New York, NY 10022
tel (212) 755 6700
email:davidoliver@
   paintlibrary.co.uk
www.paintlibrary.com
Paints and wallpapers by Neisha
Crosland, Emily Todhunter, David
Oliver and Nina Campbell (paint only)

Planning

American Architectural Directory
email:
info@americanarchitecture.com
listings for architects, interior
designers
www.architects-in-america.com
www.theinteriordesigner.com
useful online directory of suppliers
and interior design professionals

Storage

HOLD EVERYTHING
tel (800) 421 2264
www.holdeverything.com
For stores nationwide. Mail order
and retail

VITSOE
c/o Moss
146 Greene Street
New York, NY 10012
email: webenquiry@vitsoe.com
www.vitsoe.com
606 Universal shelving system

Windows

ANNA FRENCH
Classic Revivials Inc
Suite 534, Fifth floor
One Design Center Place
Boston, Mass
tel (617) 574 9030
fax (617) 574 9027
www.anna-french.demon.co.uk

ROSSO OBJEKTE
c/o Design Syntax
3525 Old Conejo Road
Suite 107
Newbury Park, CA
tel (805) 498 4747
fax (805) 498 4881
email: andreas@designsyntax.com
www.rosso-objekte.com
Modern curtain fixing systems

I would like to express my gratitude to the following people who so willingly allowed us to photograph their homes: Agnes Emery, Alex Sigmon and Alexander Jakowec, Anya van de Wetering, Barbara Davis, Bonnita Postma, Danielle Siden, Ed and Jo Howell, Freeny Yianni, Irene de Coninck, Ischa van Delft, Janie Jackson, Linda Loenen, Nathalie van Reeth, Nicolette le Pelley, Thecla Stuyling de Lange, and Tricia Foley.

A big "thank you" to all at Quadrille, especially Anne Furniss, Mary Evans, Nicky Marshall, and Sue Storey, firstly for giving me the opportunity to work on Simple Style and secondly for working together so relentlessly to produce it.

Special thanks to Hotze Eisma for his enthusiasm and good company and, of course, for taking beautiful photographs with such ease.

I am indebted to Bridget Bodoano for her words, sanity, and sense of humor; Lisa Dyer for pulling it all together at the end with verve and efficiency.

I would also like to thank Esther Jostmeyer and Jo Tyler for their assistance and companionship—making our days so enjoyable. Thanks also to Fiona at Limelight for her support and generally looking after me.

On the home front, I would like to express my gratitude to Becky for looking after my children so well, making it so much easier to work away from home; and of course a huge hug to Gum for holding the fort together and for being endlessly supportive and a great dad.

acknowledgments